I0813624

The fashion of

CLUELESS

The fashion of

CLUELESS

WRITTEN BY
COSTUME DESIGNER *Mona May*
WITH MONICA CORCORAN HAREL

SAN RAFAEL • LOS ANGELES • LONDON

Contents

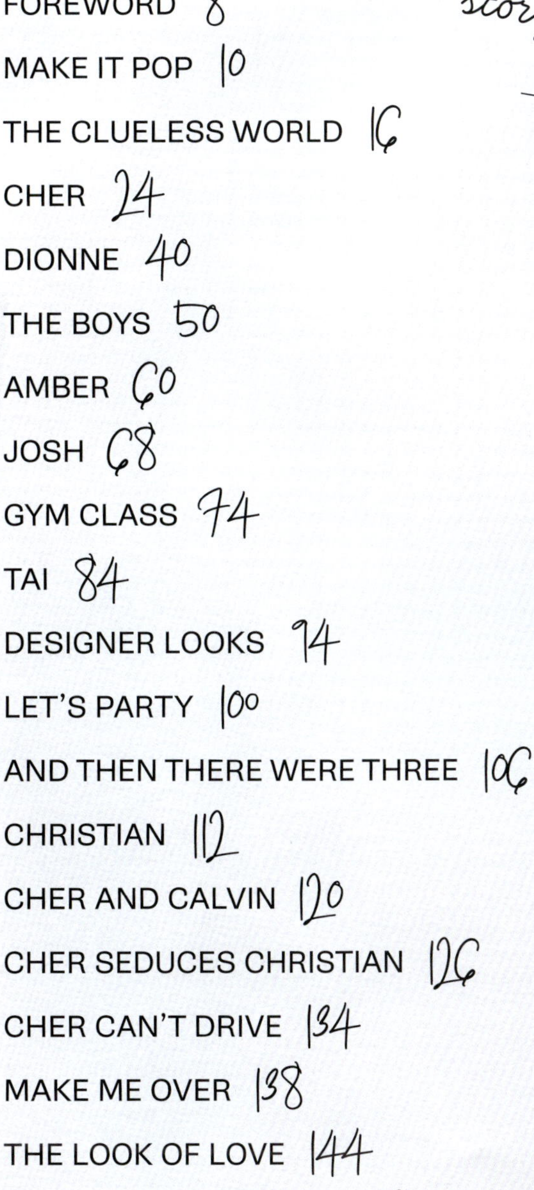

"Your clothes tell your story and you can tell a different story every day."

—MONA MAY.

A Word About Mona

One day, a producer who was putting together a film crew asked me what I thought of Mona May, the costume designer I have worked with many times. I told her that for me, the best part of making movies is working with Mona.

When my *Clueless* script was sent to studios, they unanimously said, "No." The feeling was there were too many films about "stupid teenagers" that had underperformed at the box office. Some executives told me they didn't understand what the characters were saying. But Mona got it right away. She understood the kind of world I wanted to create: a psychotically happy universe of funny, beautiful, young people whose style you'd want to copy. When I finally got a green-light to make the film, Mona and I were off to high school to see how the kids were dressing. But it soon became glaringly obvious that we would not be going for a "realistic" look because at that time, grunge wear and extremely baggy hip-hop clothing were omnipresent. And as much as I loved the music, the clothing could only be described as "schlubby." Mona felt an entirely new look would have to be created.

I noticed that kids try out many personas during their teen years, which is often expressed in their clothing choices. We had fun deciding where a character's head was at and how that would influence what they wore. For example, does Josh think he's going to lead a protest? Is Amber going to be in the ballet? Is Cher a lawyer in court presenting her closing argument? Mona's imagination went wild. We worked on her "idea board," where cut-up pictures of pants, shirts, skirts, hats, etc. were moved around to find the perfect combinations (which would've been a lot easier if my computer wardrobe app really existed).

Then there was our biggest problem. In the 1990s, the typical medium-to-low production budget was $35 million. The *Clueless* budget was $12 million, and this was before designers made deals with films to get their clothes on big movie stars (and my young actors weren't big movie stars . . . yet). Mona was going to have to be very clever to create an original look on a shoestring budget (fortunately, she is).

I relied on Mona's fearlessness. I had always been obsessed with Liza Minelli's thigh-high stockings in *Cabaret* and loved the over-the-knee socks I'd seen that had a similar but more youthful appearance. I really wanted Cher and other characters to wear them, but they were briefly marketed in the '80s and didn't catch on. I worried they'd make our girls look out of style. Mona just scoffed and said, "*We'll* decide what's in style." I so admired her boldness. It helped me trust my instincts, and it led to her changing the entire look of the '90s.

Years later, I ran into the producer who I recommended Mona to, and she agreed that she had never had such a great time on a film as she did working with Mona.

Amy Heckerling

ABOVE: While studying at the American Film Institute in Los Angeles, Heckerling jotted down all the cool expressions she heard in a notebook. "I've always been obsessed with language," she says.

OPPOSITE: Pages from Heckerling's original *Clueless* script.

2ND PINK REVISED PAGES 1/24/95

124A.

JOSH
No, no, no...I didn't mean that, I just think, you know, this is how nerds spend their time... You're young and beautiful and...

That takes her aback.

CHER
(hopeful)
And...

He realizes he called her beautiful and suddenly f awkward.

JOSH
And what?

CHER
You think I'm beautiful?

Clueless

Written

by

Amy Heckerling

Registered: WGA 5151

FIRST SHOOTING DRAFT
Oct 7, 1994

1.

GREEN REVISED PAGES 11/29/94

(7D/Oct '94) Heckerling

Clueless

Over an upbeat song we see our heroine CHER and her friend, DIONNE, a stunning, African American girl, in a montage of teenage activities. Cher is beautiful, rich and damn happy. 1

EXT. JEEP - DAY 2

Cher, Dionne and other cute kids cavort in a new jeep.

INT. SCHOOL HALLWAY - DAY 3

Cher and her pals strut down the hallways in school.

EXT. PARK - DAY

Some wacky boys toss Cher into a fountain at the park.

All seen through long lenses, hand held, smoke, dutch angles, etc.

CHER V.O.
Help! I'm trapped in a Noxema commercial.

CUT TO:

4

INT. CHER'S ROOM - MORNING

Cher is in a T-shirt and boy's boxers. She yanks squiggly rods out of her hair.

CHER V.O.
Just kidding. But I'll admit it, my life is quite full...

She turns to her computer which has her whole wardrobe programmed into it. She scans the clothing till she's picked a perfect ensemble.

CUT TO:

5 INT. CHER'S UPSTAIRS HALLWAY TO ENTRANCEWAY - DAY

Cher comes downstairs in the outfit from the computer.

CHER V.O.
... in Beverly Hills with my father, ... inent attorney...

...een Rev.	Nov. 29, 1994
...denrod Rev.	Dec. 5, 1994
... Rev.	Dec. 30, 1994
...on Rev.	Jan. 6, 1995
...y Rev.	Jan. 10, 1995
...ev.	Jan. 11, 1995
...ite Rev.	Jan. 19, 1995
...ue Rev.	Jan. 23, 1995
...llow Rev	Jan. 26, 1995

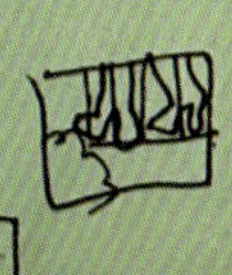

MAKE
Clothes. Popularity.
There A Problem
Here?

IT
Meet Mona May

The moment visionary director, Amy Heckerling, handed me the script for Clueless, I was in love. With the film's valuable message, with Cher and Dionne's fashions, with the infinite possibilities of a dream costume collection just waiting for me to design. In short, I was hooked.

Working on *Clueless* changed my career, my creative approach, and my life. Looking back now, thirty years later, it seems like everything I'd worked on, every experience I'd had, and every corner of the world I'd seen led me to that point.

Growing up in India, Poland, and Germany immersed me in a rich tapestry of cultures, and I soon noticed how fashion tells a story about who we are, where we come from, and who we want to be. I learned this early on when as a ten-year-old in Communist Poland, I managed to get my hands on a pair of orange bell bottoms, black clogs, and a faux fur jacket. I was obsessed with color—saffron yellows, rich teals, and vibrant pinks from my time in Calcutta—and from the minute I was handed a sewing kit, I was drawn to lush fabrics, silk kimonos, and colorful saris.

In between drawing princesses and imagining the worlds they inhabited, I styled my mother's closet and dictated the "right way" to put an outfit together. Paying close attention to how clothing could shape a personality, I developed strong creative opinions on what I would and would not wear, flatly refusing to attend my First

Communion in the traditional poufy white dress. Instead, at the tender age of twelve, I showed up in a more dignified, chic white bell-bottom pantsuit. It wasn't the last rule I'd break.

By the time I moved to New York and later to Los Angeles, I was loading up my "fashion van" with clothes to create costumes for student films and whatever projects I could land, working on music videos for Debbie Gibson and Run D.M.C. as well as various sketch comedies. But when I teamed up with Amy on a pilot about two New York City hipster girls, I knew I had found a creative soulmate. Sharing the same style, sensibility, and creative vision, we connected immediately over our mutual love of fashion. As soon as Amy began considering a creative direction for Clueless, she called to see if I was in. It would be my first studio movie, and I jumped at the chance.

A rare breed in Hollywood, Amy quickly pulled together a dream team of creatives including director of photography, Bill Pope, and production designer Steven Jordan. She was all about empowering those around her, and she truly believed I could bring her vision and her characters to life, trusting me to create a visual world for two Beverly Hills high school fashionistas, Cher and Dionne. Making them feel both aspirational and relatable would prove to be a unique design challenge: How was I going to make these characters' wardrobes high fashion while making sure they remained grounded and likeable?

If the costume designer has done their job well, you know something about the character and their story before it even unfolds. You can immediately get a sense of their background, their hopes, and their dreams. You can guess if they're sad, happy, confident, or shy. Using both my skills as a fashion designer and a costume designer—my two passions—*Clueless* was an opportunity to create a brand-new world unlike anything anyone had seen, bringing together the cultures I'd observed, my love of color, and the playful styles I'd collected from all over the world.

But there was a problem: There was no fancy PR machine and no bottomless pit of high-end designers throwing clothes at me to be featured in the movie. Remember, this was pre-digital age! Without an agent, not only did I have to negotiate my contract on my own, I also had to be scrappy. But Amy had unleashed the bottled genie in me, and the lack of resources only pushed me to get creative. I was going to make sure the clothes felt fresh and unique no matter what.

While I had carte blanche to go crazy and be myself, I quickly realized I had my work cut out for me when Amy and I scouted local high schools to get a sense of what kids were wearing. Nothing good. It was the '90s and fashion, it seemed, was on hiatus. Grunge was all the rage, but that wasn't exactly the vibe we had in mind for our cast. Ripped, baggy flannels weren't going to cut it for two vibrant, empowered, Beverly Hills fashion junkies.

Our biggest challenge then, was to create a brand-new high school universe, and the success of the film hinged on getting it right. With nothing yet existing in the real world to use as a base, we needed looks for our characters that would be fun, memorable, and lasting. To achieve this, I turned to the high fashion runways of Milan, Paris, and London for inspiration, as I imagined both Cher and Dionne might have.

OPPOSITE: Mona May in her atelier. Photo by Andrés Garzas.

We had to avoid dating them with styles that might be over before the movie was even released and the last thing we wanted to see was a pair of stuck-up snooty model types in stilettos—after all, this was high school, not New York Fashion Week. The solution was to take the chic and sometimes wild elements of the runway and make them age-appropriate and believable for teenagers. Cher had to look like the high school queen bee, without losing her teenage innocence, and Dionne had to be edgy while still fitting into the world of fashion-forward teens.

From the start, Amy and I discussed the importance of femininity—think Jane Austen meets Vivienne Westwood. She wanted to emphasize female charm and empowerment while retaining a girlish innocence. We wanted the costumes to reflect their strength, while also showcasing their vulnerability and youth. My early exposure to Italian, Japanese, Indian, and Western women helped me understand body shape, size, and variety, and most importantly the value and beauty of diverse body types. I had a global point of view that infused all of my costume choices. Mostly I drew from the elegance of the past, using elements like cap sleeves and empire waists to evoke a sense of timeless beauty. But I also made sure the clothes were modern, bright, fun, and inviting.

As a costume designer, I wanted the clothes to define the characters and the audience to be inspired to emulate their fearless sense of style. Comedy requires a delicate balance, and to avoid a cartoonish look, we had to have the actors wear the clothes rather than the other way around.

With eight weeks to prepare and a small costume budget, we had to get creative with sourcing the clothes that would make up thousands of costumes. Cher alone had sixty-three changes while Dione, Tai, and Amber had forty to fifty each. With additional supporting cast as well as extras, purchases had to be strategic—combining shopping mall finds with a few wow pieces to help tell each story and to differentiate one personality from the other. Jean Paul Gaultier's yellow plaid suit and Alaia's red dress, for example, were two crucial elements of Cher's wardrobe, but we couldn't afford to cram her closet full of designer pieces. Instead, we scoured thrift shops and tailored the vintage pieces we found to fit the actors. I worked closely with Amy to create a cohesive color palette of bright, happy tones—no browns or grays, just vibrant hues that sparkled against the California sunshine. Cher's wardrobe became a study in classic elegance, including sweater sets, pea coats, Mary Janes, and berets.

Dionne's was bolder, funkier, and more daring. Short skirts, vinyl, and leopard prints complemented her skin tone. Plus, hats. Lots of them, mainly because hats are my signature, and they were perfect for *Clueless*. Each character had a distinct look that reflected their personalities and stories.

One of the things I love most about designing costumes for movies is that it's a collaboration, and as a truly cohesive team with Amy at the helm, we discussed every aspect of the film, including the locations, sets, and fashion. From plaid suits and A-line skirts to headbands and tights, every detail mattered. And Bill Pope captured it all with his revolutionary use of the camera as a fashion lens. He did something rare, showing the viewer each outfit, head to toe. Guided by his eye, the audience was made aware of every detail: the shoes, the jewelry, even the backpacks. Steven Jordan kept the sets clean and neutral to allow the complexity of the costumes to really pop.

Costume design is an intimate process and the first thing an actor must do is undress for fittings. It's hard to hide when you're in your skivvies, so you get to know people pretty well. The cast, including Alicia Silverstone, Stacey Dash, Paul Rudd, Brittany Murphy, Donald Faison, and Breckin Meyer, were largely still unknown and they showed up unafraid, flexible, and willing to try different things.

None of us could have foreseen what happened when *Clueless* hit theaters. It was an immediate success and became a lasting cultural phenomenon. The costumes were a key part of this success with Cher's iconic yellow plaid superheroine suit and other characters' looks dominating Halloween choices, and fashion designers taking inspiration from my work. The *Clueless* look was all over the streets. *Vogue* did a feature on the costumes; *Women's Wear Daily* declared it "fashion movie of the year"; *The New York Times* called the film "an extended fashion show," and fashion magazines started profiling me. Even as Alicia, Stacey, Paul, and Brittany were catapulted to another level of fame, I never imagined that three decades later, girls, women, the LGBTQ+ community, and other fans the world over would still be influenced by the film. Teens went from wearing grunge and baggy pants to embracing the new high-fashion era the movie had ushered in. Girls began to embrace their femininity and to own their sense of style. Who could have predicted that *Clueless* would become part of the zeitgeist?

The success of *Clueless* gave me enormous confidence in my ability and in my unique voice as a designer, and it proved that fashion and storytelling can come together in a way that can change the way people view film. The costumes had supported *Clueless* in such a strong way that the clothing became a character of its own, and my vision was realized in large part due to Amy's encouragement and the incredible supporting crew. Suddenly doors flew open for me, and the phone began to ring.

In the years that followed, I was fortunate enough to work on other films that allowed me to explore and play with costume design. When Drew Barrymore called to collaborate on *Never Been Kissed*, the goal once again was to show the character's journey from shy, bookish prude, to confident, empowered female. Using costume as a language we were able to bring comedy and authenticity to Drew's character, Josie. Out came the big white feather boa for her return to school, and a pink chiffon dress in the final scene helped her fully become her true self: a strong, young woman ready to love.

For *Romy and Michele's High School Reunion*, I had even more freedom. The story involved two playful party girls who enjoyed making their own clothes, expressing *joie de vivre*, and clubbing—suddenly there was no need for innocence, and once again, I could marry current fashion and costume design. Where other designers might stay away from high fashion to avoid dating the movie, I prefer to take elements from current fashion trends and find ways to elevate them through my own vision, always with the goal of furthering the movie's story. A great costume design reveals a passion behind the choices, and I had so much fun incorporating feather boas, chain mail dresses, vinyl, and my signature vibrant colors.

As more opportunities including *Enchanted*, *The Wedding Singer*, *Stuart Little*, *A Night at the Roxbury*, and *The House Bunny* came up, each offered new challenges. Many shared a common thread: female empowerment. As a huge advocate for women, I'm so grateful to have worked on so many female-driven films. My goal has always been to empower my actors. Ultimately, the role of a costume designer is to arm actors with clothes that help them embody a character and support that character's journey.

This book illustrates how clothing can be a vehicle for storytelling and details how a costume designer can help a character evolve on screen. And for the audience who experiences the film, my goal is to show that whether it's a big feather boa or an oversized hat, clothing should invite people to explore, to experiment, and to feel confident in who they are.

Being a costume designer is an incredibly creative and fulfilling career that comes with many challenges, and I hope this behind-the-scenes look at how we brought the world of *Clueless* to life through costumes, inspires future designers and fashionistas to find their passion no matter what challenges they face, to trust their creative instincts, and to use their own unique voice.

One of the most important things to remember as a designer and perhaps, as a creator of any kind, is that while goals are helpful, you have to stay open to different outcomes. Creating costumes is unpredictable and you never know until the final fitting whether something will definitely match your original vision. Flexibility is key.

Fashion has the power to transform not just a character, but an entire film, as well as it's viewers—and if I can help budding creators, designers, and fashion lovers to see how powerful that transformation can be, then I've accomplished what I set out to do. I hope this book helps you express your own creativity, find your best self, and maybe even take a little inspiration from Cher, Dionne, and the unforgettable world of *Clueless*.

Mona May

TRANSC
The
Cluele
High Fashion
TO HIGH SCHOOL
CU L8R

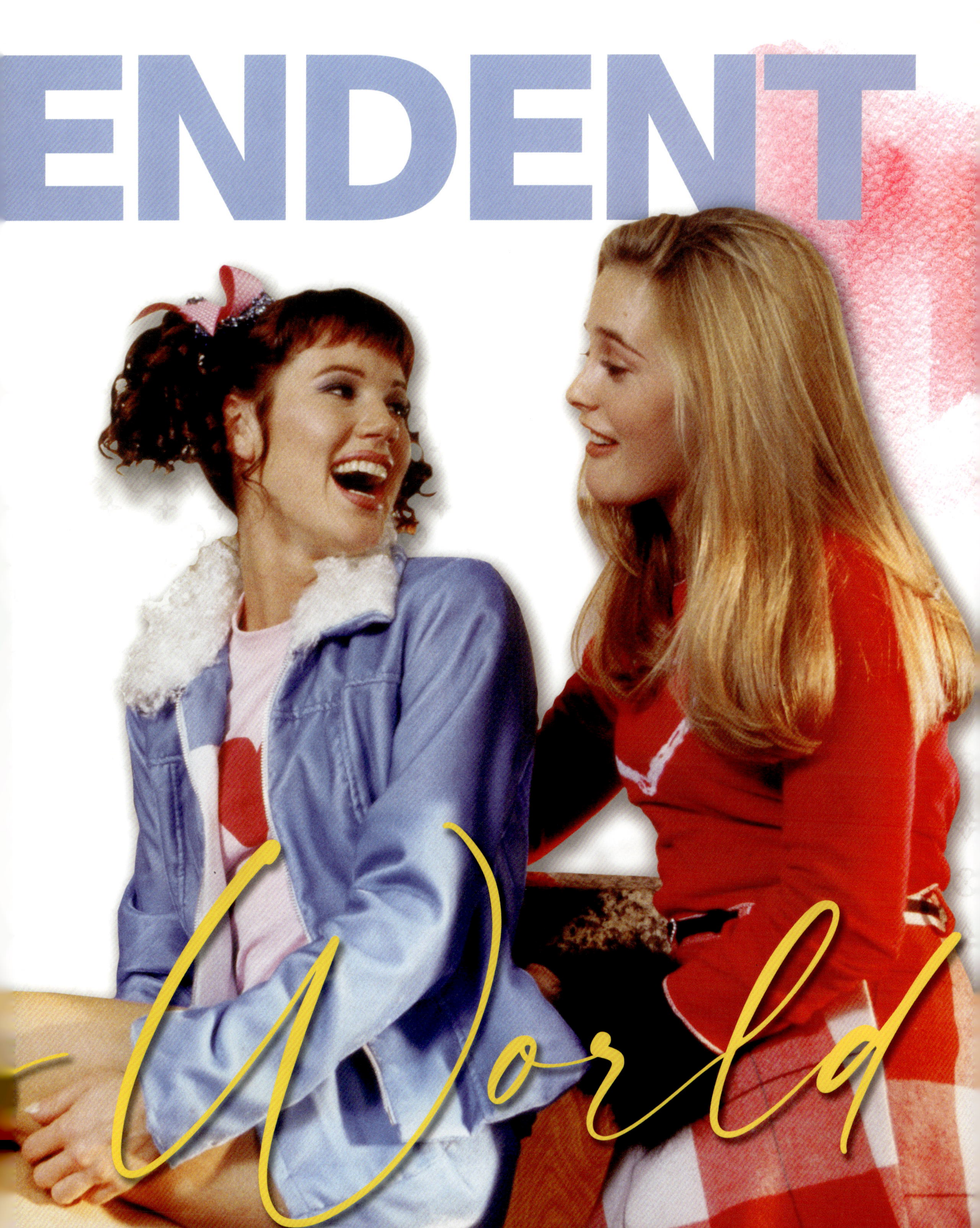
ENDENT
World

It was 1995. When *Clueless* opened in July of that summer, no one—neither its writer and director, Amy Heckerling, nor costume designer, Mona May—suspected a female-forward teen movie would put a permanent dent in pop culture, launch fashion trends, and forever change the way we say, "whatever." Heckerling had set out to write a movie about "cool kids in Beverly Hills." She looked to Jane Austen's cheeky 1815 classic *Emma* as a template. But instead, what she created was a perpetually upbeat Technicolor coming-of-age story that transcends class, race, and time. What May created was a new, sophisticated look for teens that would never go out of style. No wonder the seminal film made over $10 million on its opening weekend.

Thirty years later, *Clueless* is still relatable because it's inclusive. It continues to be aspirational because it's inspirational. Bronx-born

Heckerling based manipulative but lovable Cher Horowitz on the teenage girl she never was: "No matter what clothes Cher puts on, she already knows she looks great. She walks into a room and just assumes everyone will like her." She built a whole world around this kind-hearted heroine who uses her poise and popularity for good. The director also assembled a talented crew of creatives who could realize her vision for a modern-day comedy of manners.

"We all got immersed in this shiny bubble where Amy truly let us be artists and create a world that didn't exist," says costume designer Mona May, who was handpicked by Heckerling for her fashion background and familiarity with European designers. May worked alongside cinematographer Bill Pope, production designer Steven Jordan, and many other behind-the-scenes talents. Her choices—from Cher's iconic yellow plaid skirt suit to catwalk-worthy gym class athleisure—put *Clueless* on the map for fashion fiends everywhere, so much so that *Vogue* once called the film's costume design "the most memorable character."

"So, okay, you're probably thinking, 'Is this, like a Noxzema commercial, or what?'"

THESE PAGES: Once the teen actors all got to know each other, the *Clueless* crew liked to party as soon as Heckerling yelled, "Cut." "You heard laughter all the time," says May. "They had fun."

Q&A—Mona and Amy:

Mona: "Amy, people always ask me what inspired the clothes in *Clueless* because everyone was into Kurt Cobain and wearing grunge in the '90s."

Amy: "I didn't want it to look all dreary and sad. I wanted happy, bright colors and positivity—a world that was uplifting and stylish. So I called you."

Mona: "That's right. That world didn't exist. We went around to high schools in L.A., and everyone was wearing baggy pants and flannel shirts."

Amy: "It was so unpleasant. No wonder high school is depressing."

Mona: "I knew our girls would be into runway looks and clothes from Europe. It had to look opulent, but authentic—and totally grounded in this teen context. I had to translate high fashion into high school."

Amy: "That was the challenge. You created costume character boards for every girl. You cut up pictures from magazines, and we created outfits out of tops and bottoms. It felt like a fashion puzzle. I called Cher and Dionne's looks: 'Catholic schoolgirl on steroids'."

Mona: "There had to be some sweetness and innocence. These girls were not snooty models. We did everything in person because there was no email! I had so many tear sheets from *Vogue* and other fashion magazines. Once we decided on the looks, I had to design costumes and source clothes and borrow designer pieces. There was no PR machine back then. I literally begged Azzedine Alaia himself to use that red dress. And of course, then Alicia had to crawl on the ground in it!"

THIS PAGE: Heckerling's first feature film was the iconic *Fast Times at Ridgemont High*, which launched the careers of Sean Penn, Nic Cage, and Jennifer Jason Leigh in 1982. She did it again with Clueless, introducing new stars to the world.

Amy: "That was a real Alaia?"

Mona: "Yes! It cost more than $3,000, which was a lot of money for my budget. I was like, 'Oh my God, Alicia! Be careful on the ground!' Then, you wrote that line—'It's an Alaia!'—into the script."

Amy: "Mona, you had a vision for every character and all those racks in the fitting room. It was nonstop."

Mona: "You would come in and say, 'She needs a shiny backpack', or 'make his hair messier,' because you knew what was happening with kids that age. You let us all play and be artists. Bill Pope [the cinematographer] would capture every style detail—earrings, a hat, a backpack—with the camera. He didn't miss anything! Steven Jordan [the production designer] made sure the backgrounds were muted so the fashion popped."

Amy: "I'm lucky because everyone in our crew was totally into it—even though the budget was limited."

Mona: "I had $200,000 to come up with like a thousand costumes. And this was my first studio movie as a designer so it was a big deal. I remember at one point you told me I couldn't spend any more money, but I had to design a couture wedding dress and bridesmaid looks for the final scene."

Amy: "And Twink [who played Miss Geist] convinced me that I had to be a bridesmaid, which was kind of goofy. And then when she threw the bouquet, the girls were being so polite. I was wearing that pink suit and started shoving them to fight over it like an angry mob."

Mona: "The movie had such a gorgeous, expanded palette that ended in optimistic pink, which was perfect."

BETTY: a chic, beautiful woman

BALDWIN: a hot dude, based on the Baldwin brothers

BARNEY: a totally geeky guy

I'M AUDI: leaving now

BOINKFEST: get it on

JEEPIN': get it on in a car

HYMENALLY CHALLENGED: a virgin

SURF THE CRIMSON WAVE: menstruate

TOTAL MONET: someone who's attractive from a distance, but not when you get closer

TOE-UP: just plain ugly

Whatever: A Way with Words

Language buff Heckerling peppered her script with spicy slang only teens could say with a straight face. Some references were sourced from UCLA's 1993 official slang dictionary, while others came from Rat Pack lingo and the director's own imagination. Here are the top ten turns of phrase:

ABOVE: The life-size portrait of Cher's late mom, whom she refers to as "a total Betty," was painted by one of Twink Caplan's neighbors. "He had done a great painting of my dog, so we commissioned him," says Caplan, who played Miss Geist.

You Are What You Wear

Costume designers make dozens of calculated choices with every outfit. They convey a character's inner emotions, identity, status, and interests through clothes and accessories. Take Cher, a 16-year-old who wears a literal *suit* in the first scene like she's a CEO. Clearly, she's confident about her perch in the high school hierarchy. May added femininity with Cher's over-the-knee stockings, capped sleeves, empire waists, and white Mary Janes. Cher's polished look sums up her ambition. One look and you just know she gets what she wants. "Your clothes tell your story, and you can tell a different story every day," says May, who asks herself, "Who am I today?" before she steps into her own closet. May has a few techniques up her sleeve that you can try at home.

• COLOR HAS ENERGY: Happy characters wear bright shades that match their mood. May opts for more somber tones like gray and black to show that someone is sad or feeling insecure. "I can show the arc of a character through the colors or prints she wears in a movie," says May. "When Cher realizes that she's superficial, she wears more muted clothes that show her being reflective."

• FABRIC AND SILHOUETTE SAY A LOT: Tailored jackets with strong shoulders telegraph power, while organic shapes allude to softness. May likes to mix both silhouettes to show that characters can be complex. Textured fabrics like boucle and tweed also signify strength, while sheer shirts and silk pieces convey approachability.

• FIT SPEAKS TO LUXURY: "Someone with clothes that fit her body perfectly definitely gets custom-made pieces or alterations," says May, who encourages everyone to find a trusted tailor. "People don't realize that it doesn't cost a lot to have a dress taken in or pants cuffed to fit perfectly."

CONF

Fashion
AS AN ART FORM
"As if!"

I want to do something for humanity.

Cher Horowitz broke the mold on teen-next-door movie tropes. She was popular, but inclusive. Stunning, yet never stuck-up. Entitled *and* generous. In Cher's own words, "I actually have a way normal life for a teenage girl." As if! Heckerling always envisioned the Beverly Hills high schooler as a misguided but earnest good girl—the kind of friend who shows up on your doorstep with an extra-large pizza after a breakup. "Cher's motives were pure—even if she was misdirected. She wanted to uplift people, make them cool and confident so they would be accepted and loved," she says.

To convey Cher's character through costumes, May chose a colorful, upbeat palette and tailored separates like structured blazers and crisp button-downs. She added girly accessories like headbands, a fur pen, and Mary Janes to nod at Cher's innocence and femininity. May says, "Even though she's only sixteen, she knows that clothes make a big impression."

ABOVE, OPPOSITE: With hundreds of costumes to track from scene to scene, May's team used "continuity Polaroids" to rigorously detail each look, including jewelry like Cher's earrings and the black beret seen on the opposite page.

Q&A - Mona and Alicia:

MONA: "Alicia, what do you remember from our fittings?"

ALICIA: "I tried on clothes for days and days and days! I was like, 'Why are we doing this?' But of course, I understood when I saw the movie."

MONA: "Well, you had sixty-three costumes! You brought a softness to Cher. With those high-fashion clothes, she could have come across as bitchy instead of lovable and charming."

ALICIA: "Thank you. Her looks were so over-the-top. I mean, who wears high heels to high school? And those matching outfits? The beret? But somehow, it all worked because you and Amy had a vision."

MONA: "We created something brand new that wasn't happening at that time. I think that's why it has staying power and never goes out of style. Did playing Cher and wearing all those designer looks have any impact on your own style?"

ALICIA: "If I'm being super honest, I never had any interest in clothes even though I knew that my costumes were an artistic and essential piece of the puzzle. I was more interested in saving the world than getting dressed."

MONA: "I remember. And you're still an activist."

ALICIA: "But when I turned forty, I started to appreciate fashion as an art form. And now, I can be eco-friendly and make conscious fashion choices. I don't have to sacrifice my desire to look pretty as a woman."

FUN FACT:
Like Cher, director and New Yorker Heckerling failed her California driver's test . . . many times. Maybe she needed a more "capable" outfit?

LEFT: Alicia Silverstone and Jeremy Sisto had already acted together in the film *Hideaway*, so playing friends was no stretch for them.

MONA: "It's funny that you weren't interested in fashion back then because you were the one who wore all the major designers like Jean Paul Gaultier, Alaia, and Calvin Klein."

ALICIA: "I did like that little green dress I wore with the matching purse. And the movie inspired people to play with clothes and even to become designers. Mona, you would not believe the amount of people who tell me they got into fashion because of Cher."

MONA: "And you, too. You brought Cher to life."

The Near Miss

Ironically, Cher's yellow plaid skirt suit designed by Jean Paul Gaultier almost didn't make the cut. "I thought blue would look so good on Alicia's blond hair," May says. "So, I set out to find a blue plaid suit. As I was shopping, I also found a cool red plaid suit. Since I'm a huge fan of Vivienne Westwood designs, I grabbed it! In the last hours of shopping, I spotted the yellow Jean Paul Gaultier. It wasn't the right color, I thought. Yellow usually doesn't look good on blondes, but I had to at least get Alicia to try it on. In the fitting room the magic begins. I was sure the blue suit would be perfect, but though it was very pretty, it didn't work. Next, we tried the red one and Amy was like, 'No, it's too Xmass'y!'"

Clueless

Dionne & Cher
1st Day of School

What would Cher wear on her first day of school? I started imagining how to translate the original Catholic school girl uniform to Cher's Beverly Hills world.

The scene takes place in the school quad with a lot of trees, and we see students crossing in front of Cher. She's going to have to stand out against the green background. And it's the first time we meet her character on screen — it has to be FABULOUS!!

When Alicia stepped out of the changing room in that yellow Jean Paul Gaultier plaid suit we gasped! She looked ELECTRIC!! Exactly what a queen B should wear on her first day of school! And now it's fashion history!!!"

I get up, I brush my teeth, and I pick out my school clothes.

OMG! That Closet!

Cher's digitized closet not only spits out the perfect outfit but also revolves to reveal her entire wardrobe. For Heckerling, the prescient idea was born out of frustration: "I hate trying things on and looking in the mirror. Is this stupid? Or too cheesy?" Heckerling had a friend who uploaded photos of his wine collection into his computer, so she applied the concept to fashion. "I love that a computer helps you get dressed in the morning. How cool is that?" (Talk about a precursor to A.I.) Thirty years later, apps for digitizing your closet and pairing separates abound. "Of course, Amy revolutionized how we get dressed without even trying," says May.

OPPOSITE: After some retail therapy, Cher heads home with fashion loot in telltale logo bags from Tiffany, Fendi, Barney's, and Giorgio Beverly Hills.

Clueless
Weekend
Pismo

The *Clueless* Continuum

Teen movies don't typically inspire runway looks, editorial fashion spreads, advertising campaigns, and Halloween costumes—consistently over thirty years, no less. Designers, from Versace to Christian Dior, have sent creative reinterpretations of *Clueless* costumes down the runway as homage. Kendall Jenner once said that Karl Lagerfeld, ahem, lifted the idea of the chic gym accessories for his Chanel water bottle holders. Former Calvin Klein creative director Francisco Costa reissued the itty-bitty white slip dress Cher's dad calls "pyjamas" in 2010, while Alice + Olivia-founder Stacey Bendet once said she includes plaid miniskirts in most fall collections, thanks to May's vision.

"Every single Halloween, I get pictures sent to me and they're always in the yellow plaid outfit," says Silverstone, who reprised her '90s looks as Cher for a recent Marc Jacobs campaign. Fans like Kim Kardashian and Lupita Nyong'o have recreated Cher and Dionne's looks. Iggy Azalea devoted her "Fancy" music video to the film with a modern take on the movie. "The best form of flattery is imitation," says May. "When I see Taylor Swift wearing a Dior dress in that iconic yellow plaid to an awards show, I get chills."

OPPOSITE: Model Agyness Deyn for House of Holland's London Ready to Wear line. Photo by CAMERA PRESS/ Anthea Simms.

OPPOSITE RIGHT: Everyone dressed up for the *Clueless* 30th anniversary screening at Cinespia in Hollywood Forever Cemetery!

ABOVE LEFT: Donald Faison's daughter dressed as Dionne for Halloween.

ABOVE RIGHT: Taylor Swift at the 2024 MTV Video Music Awards. Photo by Image Press Agency.

ABOVE: Mona May owns almost fifty fedoras—and gets recognized on the street for her signature style. "I don't feel like myself if I'm not wearing a hat. It's my fashion security blanket," she says. Photo by Kiino Villand.

What's Your Signature?

Leading ladies have to stand out on screen—and costume designers know a trusty style trademark sets them apart. (Think about Cher and her headbands or Dionne and her crazy hats.) "Maybe it's a red lip or a fedora. Pick a style statement that identifies you and makes you feel confidently yourself," says May. Here are three shortcuts to finding your signature:

• Stay in uniform. A consistent style like jumpsuits, monochromatic separates, or faded jeans with a classic button-down and loafers can easily become your go-to look.

• Find a stand-out accessory—chunky gold earrings, sleek oversized sunglasses, knee-high riding boots—that works for you and wear that accent on repeat.

• A distinct hairstyle like a tousled topknot, braids, or beachy waves can become your calling card. Likewise, a commanding red pout never goes unnoticed. Same goes for lush sky-high lashes. If you prefer a more natural face, focus on a power brow.

ACCESSORIES
RED LIPS
CUTE PURSE

EDGY

INSPIRE YOUR
Fashion Sense
one
"So check it"

"She's my friend because we both know what it's like to have people be jealous of us."

When Cher and Dionne stride through the high school quad in synchronized plaid and speak in shorthand, you just know they're BFFs. And throughout the movie, their bond and boundaries remain intact. They tell each other hard truths—"Would you call me selfish?" "No, not to your face."—and never compete for popularity. (Take note, mean girls.) Cher and Dionne are empowered as individuals but stronger together.

"I just love that we were so confident in our friendship," says Stacey Dash, who played Dionne. Inspired by their sweet, symbiotic relationship, May outfitted Dionne in 45 ensembles that complemented, but never overpowered, Cher's style. She also highlighted her edgy attitude: "Dionne was more experienced than Cher, so she wore more provocative clothes and showed off her midriff. She had swagger." Dash also showed up to set on the first day with her signature box braids, which landed her a slot on *Essence* magazine's "Most Iconic Celebrity Braids of All Time" list.

BELOW: While every character has a distinct look, there's visual synergy in each scene–like the varying shades of red on each girl.

OPPOSITE: Dionne's floral Dolce & Gabbana crop top was one of Dash's favorite looks.

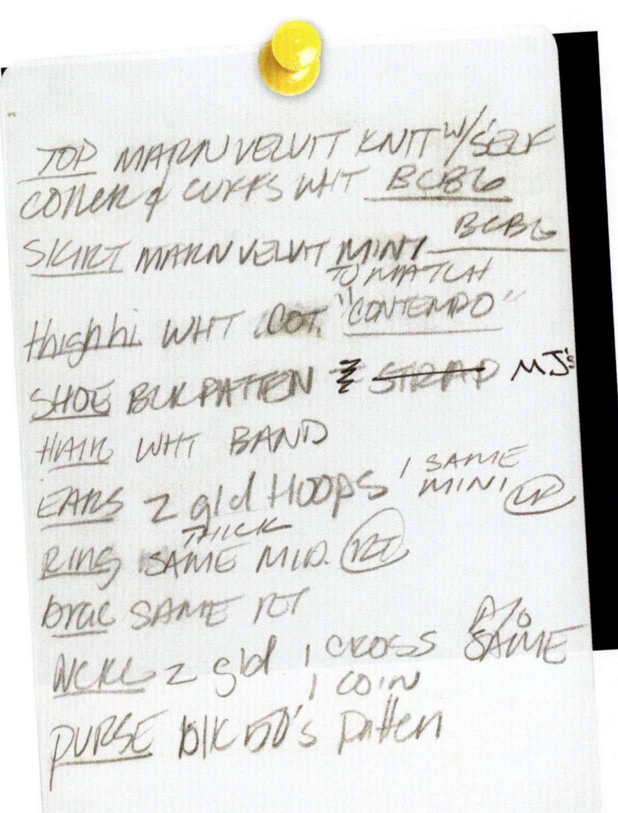

THESE PAGES: "I had so much fun with Dionne because she wore sexier looks and showed a little more skin than Cher," says May. "I loved every single costume," says Dash.

Q&A–Mona and Stacey:

MONA: "Stacey, I remember our first day together. You already loved fashion. You were so excited when we started going through the looks for Dionne."

STACEY: "As a teenager growing up in the '80s in the Bronx, I was a hardcore punk rocker with a shaved head so that was part of my aesthetic. When I walked into my first fitting with you and saw all those racks, I was like, 'Here we go!'"

MONA: "I could push the envelope with you. I put you in that Dr. Suess hat or the vinyl mini skirt because I knew you could pull it off. You were so self-assured."

STACEY: "I always say it wouldn't be *Clueless* without the genius of Mona May. The wardrobe was a main character. And every look helped me build Dionne. I made a lot of my acting choices around the wardrobe choices. For example, in the wedding scene, you made me that spectacular outfit and I thought, 'What would Dionne do with her hair?' Put flowers in her braids because she wants to stand out—even if it's not her wedding."

MONA: "You stood out for so many girls, too. When I do talks about the film at schools, these young women get emotional about seeing an empowered African American girl living in Beverly Hills in that role. It meant so much to them."

STACEY: "I hear young girls tell me that it helped them get through school and conceive the dreams they wanted to achieve. They saw a whole new realm of possibility when they saw Dionne, thanks to you and Amy. It's epic!"

MONA: "How did playing Dionne shape who you are now?"

STACEY: "I come from nothing. Both of my parents were drug addicts. When I read the script about a rich girl in high school with two loving, successful parents, I was like, 'I want to be her.' And it was so fulfilling to play Dionne. I still want to be Dionne. I'm so grateful."

MONA: "Me too. I gained so much confidence from working on *Clueless*."

STACEY: "My daughter Lola was inspired by Dionne, too. She wears hats and loves to go thrifting."

MONA: "What about you? How did playing Dionne inspire your fashion sense?"

STACEY: "I embraced leopard! I have a pair of four-inch leopard Christian Louboutins that I bought in Paris over ten years ago. They're stunning. I take such good care of them. And every time I put them on, I think of you."

How to Marry Modern with Vintage

Dionne seamlessly paired thrift-store finds with high fashion—like a hard-edged red vintage vinyl mini skirt with a feminine, cap-sleeved Jill Stuart sweater. "You can make a contemporary look totally unique by adding a piece from another era. Plus, you're being sustainable by thrifting," says May, who shares her top tips for mixing the old with the new.

• Don't overdo it with one decade: Too many pieces and accessories from the same era can make you look like a movie extra in a period movie, says May. Instead, vary your vintage looks. A thrifted 1940s peplum velvet blazer elevates a simple modern shift.

• Look for separates: Bypass the vintage basics, which are probably more worn out, for interesting separates. A bright, geometric-print Pucci blouse from the 1960s looks great with a current pair of faded jeans; a vintage leather trench adds grit to a feminine look pulled from today's racks.

• Show off your natural shape: Different decades in fashion highlight different body types. "Look for clothes that make your assets pop," says May. Case in point: the '70s was all about slinky looks like DVF wrap dresses and lean jumpsuits, while the '50s celebrated the bombshell figure with pencil skirts and snug sweaters. Find the era that works best for your figure.

ABOVE: You can almost hear the "awww" as matchmakers Cher and Dionne watch Miss Geist and Mr. Hall flirt at school.

GOLDEN

Hat Trick

May never leaves her house without her favorite finishing touch: "For me, a hat just completes the outfit." Dionne wears twenty-five hats in *Clueless*, but most fans call out her layer cake-like topper embellished with a patent brim and a huge camellia, designed by New York milliner Kokin. Granted, that look is *extra*. If you're uncertain about wearing a hat, May advises you start with a fedora. "It's got a smaller brim so it's not so dramatic," she says. Berets, too, are easy to wear. "I even like a cool, brightly-colored baseball hat," says May. "Right now, I'm wearing a red one that says 'Stay Grounded.'"

"The hat was my post-modern take on Chanel. I wanted it to be futuristic but also have that very '50s shape, because Audrey Hepburn was my fantasy muse at the time."

-KOKIN

OPPOSITE: May made sure Dionne's first-day-of-school outfit didn't clash or compete with Cher's yellow plaid by creating a black-and-white palette with a splash of bright red. The vinyl lapels on her jacket tie into the brim of her Dr. Seuss-inspired hat.

SM
The

OTH
Unique Style
Boys

The *Clueless* world really comes alive as a West Coast teen biosphere when we see first see Cher at high school—and meet the guys she tolerates. There's smooth, fast-talkin' Murray, a.k.a. Dionne's boyfriend played by Donald Faison, and Jeremy Sisto as Elton, an arrogant, moody rich kid with a crush on Cher and lots of designer sweaters. "Usually, boys just look generic in teen movies, but I wanted these characters to each have their own unique style," says May. Her efforts paid off. Breckin Meyer, who stole hearts as sweet skater-stoner Travis, recalls the moment he got his 'fit. "The clothes felt so organic to my role that the minute I put them on, there was like no acting required."

"Rollin' with the homies."

THESE PAGES: The actors bonded on set and still check in with each other. "Back in the day, I stayed with Breckin or Donald when I was in L.A.," says Rudd.

Q&A—Mona and Jeremy, Donald, and Breckin:

MONA: "Jeremy, I had so much fun with Elton because he loved fashion. What did you think of him when you first read the script?"

JEREMY: "Elton was the character I wanted to play. Not because he was rich, popular, and hot, but because, while his perspective was so ridiculous, it was also somehow the most honest. He was unabashed about the priorities of his eco-system and . . . like . . . don't you know who his father is?!!"

MONA: "You guys all got so tight on the set. I loved that."

JEREMY: "I spent a lot of time with Breckin and Donald. I remember us going on a ride at Universal Studios, one of those big-screen-moving-seat kinda rides. I was having so much fun, and I could hear them laughing too, so I thought we were in it together. Afterward I turned to them and they were laughing at me, at how much fun I was having. Jerks."

MONA: "Donald, you had to look super stylish as Murray because you were with Dionne. She would not go out with a slob."

DONALD: "Let me be honest. No girls dated me until after *Clueless*. Everything changed once they saw me as this stylish dude, Murray. I learned so much about wearing bright colors and what looked good on me from you. My whole fashion sense changed. I started dressing like Murray after the movie came out, too."

MONA: "I'm glad I helped you get dates! Why do you think *Clueless* is still such a hit?"

DONALD: "It wasn't just about rich teenagers in Beverly Hills. The movie is about these kids trying to freaking come of age and understand that they're not the center of the world. It's called *Clueless*, but by the end, these kids are on their way to being good people."

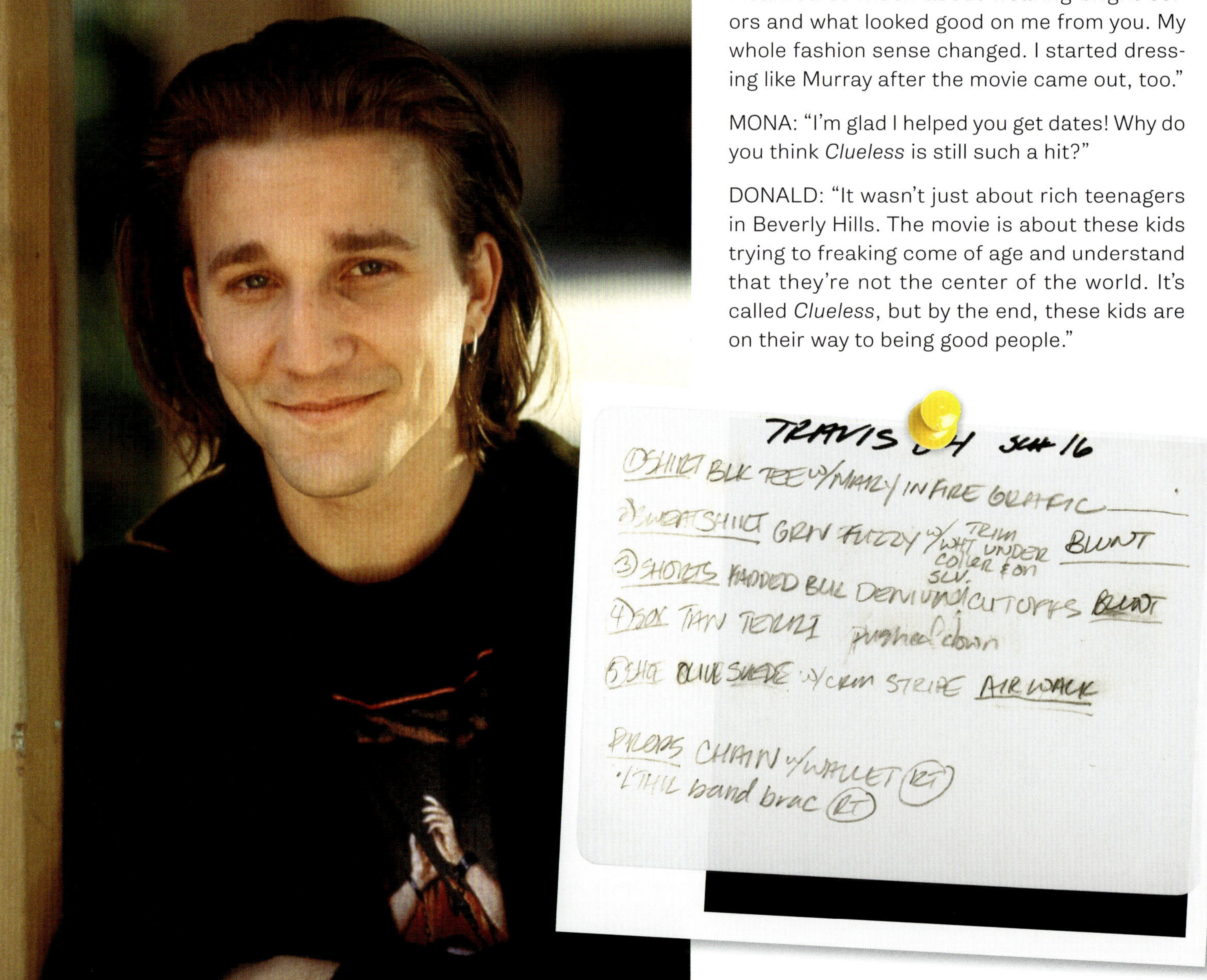

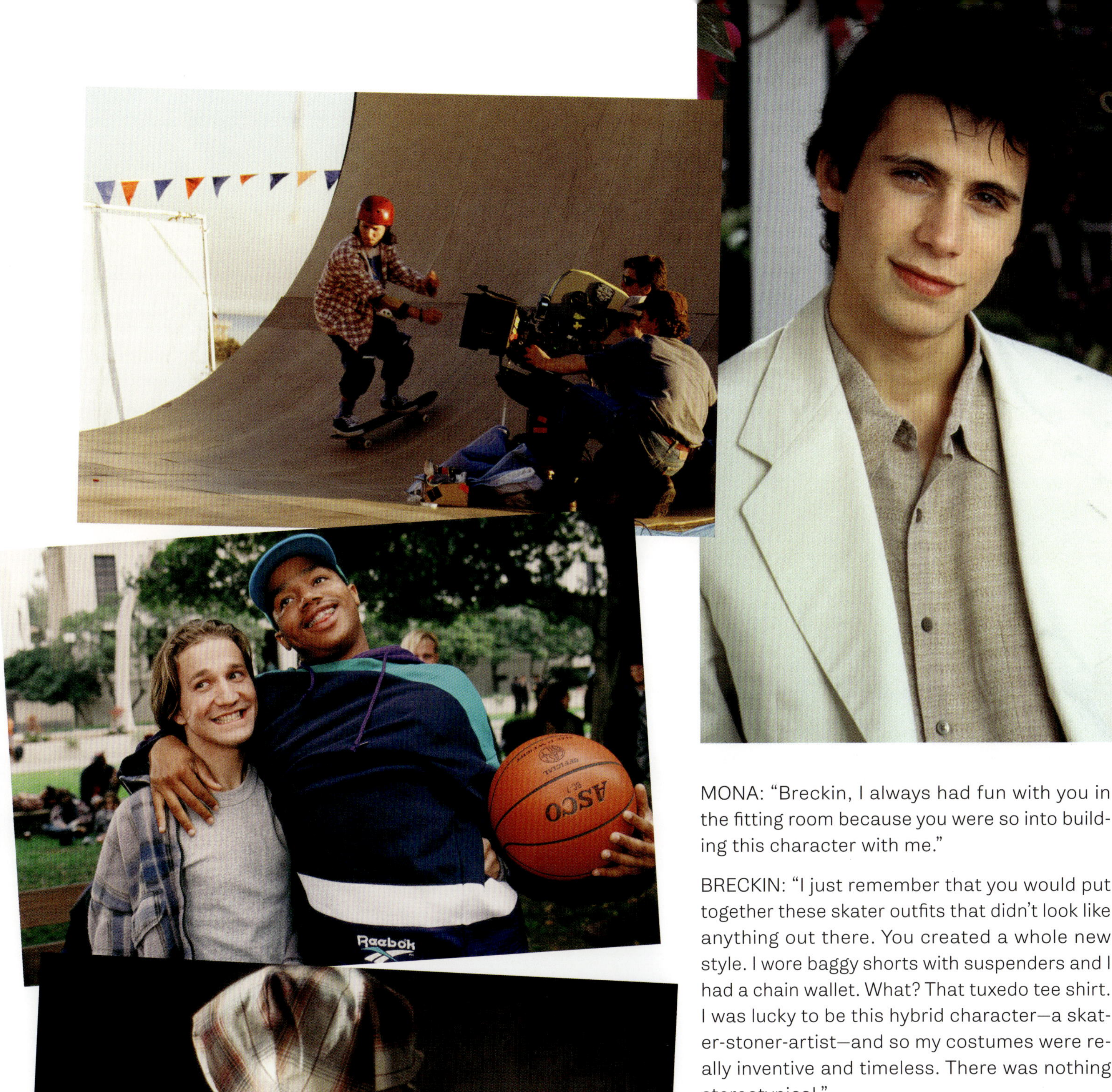

MONA: "Breckin, I always had fun with you in the fitting room because you were so into building this character with me."

BRECKIN: "I just remember that you would put together these skater outfits that didn't look like anything out there. You created a whole new style. I wore baggy shorts with suspenders and I had a chain wallet. What? That tuxedo tee shirt. I was lucky to be this hybrid character—a skater-stoner-artist—and so my costumes were really inventive and timeless. There was nothing stereotypical."

MONA: "In your opinion, what made *Clueless* a cult film?

BRECKIN: "The script, the costumes, and the casting. But it's also very, very relatable at its core. Everyone has faked it, whether you're at a new school or a new job, or in a new relationship. So we're all clueless at some point in our lives and wondering, 'How the hell do I get people to like me—or love me?' There's big wish fulfillment, too. Meaning, 'I wish I had [those] clothes and could look like that.'"

Style Guide: Chic and Cool Costumes for Cliques

"I don't want to be a traitor to my generation and all, but I don't get how guys dress today," says Cher as she ticks off the social circles at her high school. With hundreds of adolescent extras, May faced the task of making every clique shine individually.

In an opening scene, a group of cheerleaders in white sweaters and black pleated skirts pass, with one of them sporting a rhinoplasty bandage on her nose. "That was all Amy. She knew that nose jobs would be normalized at a Beverly Hills high school," she says.

The "loadies", or stoner-skaters, who hang out on the grassy knoll, stand out for their Cali streetwear: baggy pants, oversized flannel shirts, and sunglasses to disguise bleary eyes. "That was not my personal style at the time, though friends used to say that my look was 'Eddie Vedder at a funeral,'" says Meyer.

Murray's crew of guys sport jeans that sag to show off boxers, backwards hats, and labels of the moment like Adidas. "A lot of people don't know that wearing your jeans like that came from prison. I pulled mine down even lower," says Faison. "California kids are always on the forefront of fashion," says May.

THESE PAGES: Heckerling envisioned a colorful high school ecosystem where stoners and jocks and nerds and cheerleaders all swam upstream together.

The Male Flex

Guys often overlook accessories. But really, there's no easier way to spice up a look than with an accent. In *Clueless*, Murray had his gold Superman logo chain and a Kangol for every occasion. Travis heightened his look with suspenders and skater-approved Airwalk sneakers, while Elton wore a shiny Rolex watch worth more than a compact car. "Guys can play with accessories—like jewelry and shoes and hats—just like women do. And it's unexpected on a man, so there's more impact," says May, who loves to put actors in signet rings, bold watches, and hats.

DRAM
COMMITTED TO
Fashion
adidas
adidas

MATIC
Amber
"Whatever"

Do you prefer fashion victim or ensembly-challenged?

For Amber, every high school hallway is a Paris runway. She wears over thirty outrageous outfits in *Clueless*. Whether it's a fiery red sailor suit with matching shoes and hat or fatigues accented with faux-fur leopard print and a camo backpack, Amber takes a theme to dizzying heights. Who else would show up to homeroom at 9 a.m. decked out in marabou feathers? "Cher and Amber were fashion rivals and frenemies, so it was fun to have them try to outdo each other with their outfits," says May. Elisa Donovan, who played Amber, recalls that everyone on set would anticipate her grand entrances. "Every day, it was like, 'What will Amber be wearing next?' and Mona's costumes never disappointed them."

THESE PAGES: Amber managed to pivot her style from debutante to Pippi Longstocking to sailor girl to head-to-toe-camo—all in one week!

1-4
1-8
1-12
1-3
1-7
1-11
1-2
1-6
1-10

Q&A—Mona & Elisa:

MONA: "What I loved about Amber was that she committed to fashion. She was always dedicated to a look. I had so much fun creating her wardrobe."

ELISA: "Me, too. I loved that she was unafraid to be her true self and forge her own path. I was like, 'Oh, she's my kind of gal.' I got really enmeshed in Amber. I would drive around Beverly Hills and think, 'Maybe that's her house.' I was scaffolding a full person."

MONA: "It showed. You were so playful and game for anything in the fitting room. We would talk about Amber's look and then exaggerate it. She was that girl who wears all of her accessories at once. You were fearless!"

ELISA: "That's because I trusted you, Mona. I never had to worry. You were at the top of your craft. I knew we could create this character together."

MONA: "What did you think of Amber when you first read the script?"

ELISA: "I knew exactly who she was from my junior high. I can't say her name. But I also had to find a place of loving Amber, right? So, I based her on myself, too. And really, Amber just wanted Cher to accept her."

MONA: "The character is still beloved because of you. I remember that day in the fitting room where I put you in the red sailor hat. Then, I found that crazy dollar sign and added it, too."

ELISA: "Oh my God, I wish I had that sailor hat. But what I really want is the fatigues outfit. Those combat boots? I loved the whole silhouette of that look. It also really informed the character for me. In acting school, they tell you to think about what shoes your character would wear. You helped me find Amber with every pair of shoes!"

MONA: "I knew that Amber really wanted to be seen. In one scene, she wears that knit Missoni-inspired outfit with the Pippi Longstocking braids. They put pipe cleaners in your hair! Amber used fashion to get attention and to role play with different looks."

Style Guide: Anatomy of the Debate Scene Look

We first meet Amber when she and Cher debate public policy. Her look in this classroom scene establishes her fashion philosophy: More is more. "Coco Chanel said, 'Take one accessory off before you leave the house.' But Amber does the opposite," says May, who applauds this character for her bold choices.

Amber tries to outdo Cher with her own headband, edged in black marabou feathers. "They are fashion rivals, so I wanted to show how they face off with accessories," says May.

May took a black cardigan and added marabou feather trim to give Amber a dramatic silhouette. She basically added a boa, the pinnacle of over-the-top style, to a sweater. How to dress up a simple sweater without the fanfare? Add a silk scarf or a vintage brooch, suggests May.

Beneath the dramatic sweater, Amber wore a white tee shirt paired with Levi's 501 jeans. "Amber knew how to elevate a basic high school look," says May. "She looks like she's ready to go clubbing in Hollywood!"

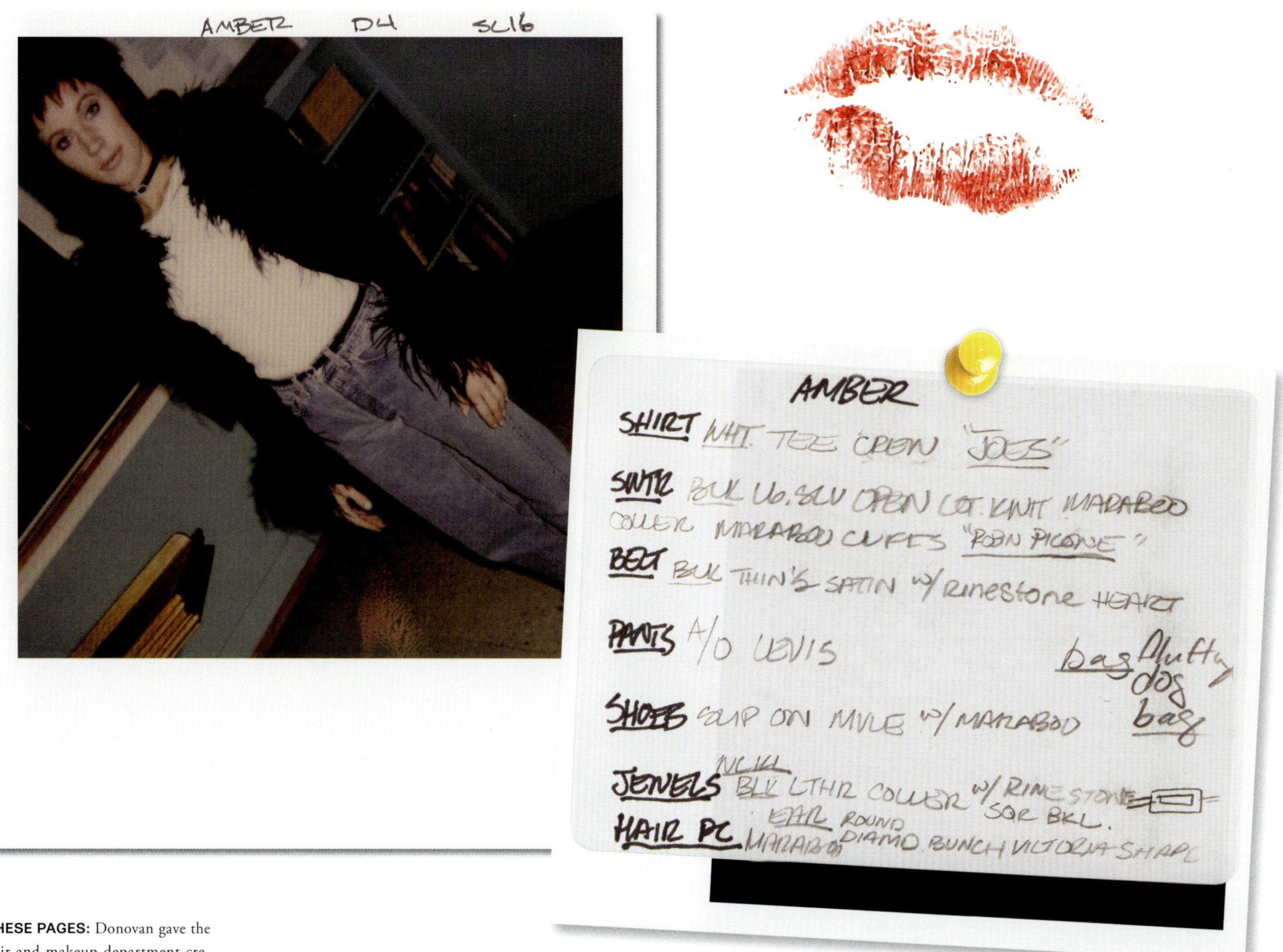

THESE PAGES: Donovan gave the hair and makeup department creative license to cut her bangs and play up her eyes. But she insisted on wearing her favorite brown lipstick in every scene.

Uh-oh. Overkill!

"Do you prefer fashion victim or ensemble-y challenged?" Cher asks Amber in *Clueless*. Granted, the striking redhead may have outdone herself with every over-the-top outfit, but she wore each style like it was part of her being and made it her own. "You never want your clothes to wear you. A fashion victim can't walk in her heels or get out of a car in her dress," says May who has five tips for avoiding the dreaded label.

• GO EASY ON LOGOS: Head-to-toe luxury monograms doesn't say much about your own personal style—especially since you're wearing someone else's initials.

• AVOID ILL-FITTING ANYTHING: A tight top that constantly needs to be tugged back in place or pants that puddle at the cuff are a dead giveaway for style homicide.

• FEAR FADS: Runway trends can expire faster than fat-free yogurt. Remember the $2,750 trash bag pouch? Stick with classic, timeless styles like Cher's cap sleeve sweaters, empire waists, and pea coats.

• CONSIDER RED CARPET VS. REALITY: Be inspired by the celebrity looks at premieres and award shows, but don't mimic them. Your goal is to create a style that reflects *you*.

• DRESS THE PART: You wouldn't show up at a night club in a business suit, so don't interview for a job in a tube dress. Get dressed with context in mind.

STYLE

ADVERTISE YOUR
Identity

NTIAL

Josh

"So, the flannel shirt deal. Is that a nod to the crispy Seattle weather, or you trying to stay warm in front of the refrigerator?"

Paul Rudd credits *Clueless* with his career. In fact, the role of Cher's smug, Nietzsche-reading stepbrother, Josh, landed him his next big part alongside Leonardo DiCaprio in *Romeo + Juliet*. It also made him an intergenerational heart-throb: "These girls come up to me and say, 'We just watched *Clueless*. My mom loves you!'" That totally tracks. With his sky-blue eyes and signature smirk, Josh is the movie's sexy moral compass who nudges Cher to put philanthropy before retail therapy. "Paul was adorable and really smart, so he could embody Josh," says Heckerling of the character's wit and interest in social justice.

Thanks to May's intentional costuming, we all swoon when he shows up onscreen in a tee shirt supporting breast cancer research. Josh is our sensitive everyman. Watching the verbal fisticuffs and flirtation between the step-siblings made everyone long for Josh and Cher to quit bickering and kiss already. So much so that we exhale when Cher finally utters "I am majorly, totally, butt crazy in love with Josh!" Then, we all want to shout, "Duh. So are we!"

LEFT: Remarkably, Rudd was actually a fan of Nietzsche and a Greenpeace supporter when they shot the film. "I'm kinda playing me," he says.

FUN FACT:
Heckerling's own married grandparents were step-siblings, like Josh and Cher.

Q&A—Mona & Paul:

MONA: "It's been 30 years, Paul. We were all so young. Do you remember your audition?"

PAUL: "All I know is that I was just out of school and didn't have much experience. I auditioned a few times, and every time I went in, there were more people in the room. That was a good sign."

MONA: "Did you ever imagine the movie would become so iconic?

PAUL: "No, and it's so funny because I remember we all went to a bar one day after a table read. We were talking about the high school movies we watched growing up—and how they were a huge part of our lives. Like the John Hughes movies. And I think one of us said, 'Wouldn't it be cool if our movie worked and became a high school movie everyone loves?'"

MONA: "I think part of what makes people gravitate to *Clueless* is its innocence. The characters were in high school, and they weren't malicious."

PAUL: "There was a real lack of cynicism. Amy writes these characters that seem to be one way, but then you realize that they're multi-dimension. They're teenagers who are sweet and supportive. There is so much humanity in that movie."

MONA: "We were doing high fashion with the girls and everything was hyped up. But you were an anchor, such a grounding character. You brought so much of yourself to the role."

PAUL: "Ha. I brought my tee shirts like the Amnesty International one. I think I wore my own boots, too. I had that KU [Kansas University] hat because I went there. And you put me in a breast cancer awareness tee shirt and that one from a 688 club in Georgia. People still ask me about that tee shirt."

MONA: "Your clothes, especially your tee shirts, really told the story of who you were and what you stood for. But sadly, we don't have any of the costumes."

PAUL: "The looks you created are so iconic and recognizable that they may even end up on some auction site."

MONA: "I hope so. But still, I'm glad we have these amazing memories."

The Tao of the Tee

No piece of clothing sums you up as succinctly as a graphic tee. Whether it's emblazoned with a Lana Del Rey logo or a political cause, everyone gets your point. The sartorial staple actually dates back to WWII, when the military advertised platoons on plain white shirts. (FYI: Writer F. Scott Fitzgerald first put the term "t-shirt" in print in a 1920 novel.) Throughout *Clueless*, Josh dons graphic tees that reveal his political leanings, music preferences, and feminist sensitivity. "We revealed a lot of his personality and interests through his shirts," says May. Inclined to advertise your identity with a cool tee? May suggests men do like Josh and layer it with a button-down shirt or a well-cut blazer. For women, tuck a concert tee into tailored jeans and add a chic belt, or pair a well-worn t-shirt with a tailored suit and heels. "I love to mix casual clothes and formal wear. You can make a tee shirt look elegant with a tuxedo," says May.

SPO
A Fashion
FORCE FIELD
Gym

RTY
Class

Sweatshirts? No way. Tube socks? As if. When Cher, Dionne and classmates hit gym class, the high school tennis court becomes a fashion force field. Now, May's handiwork stands out for its foresight: She created chic athletic wear twenty years ahead of its time. *People* magazine put it this way: "We can pretty much thank Cher and Dionne for inventing the athleisure trend, no?" May says she knew the girls needed elevated, sporty looks. "They would never wear plain, old track suits," says the costume designer, who created spandex onesies, water bottle holders, and phone purses for the scene. Actress and comedian Julie Brown, who played phys-ed teacher Miss Stoeger, didn't get the memo. "I was literally in a big sweatshirt with a whistle, and the other girls looked so glamorous," she recalls. "I didn't even get to wear make up!"

"Miss Stoeger, my plastic surgeon doesn't want me doing any activity where balls fly at my nose."

THESE PAGES: Heckerling named the school Bronson Alcott High School after "one of the first big feminists who thought women should get an education"–Amos Bronson Alcott. His daughter Louisa May would go on to write *Little Women*.

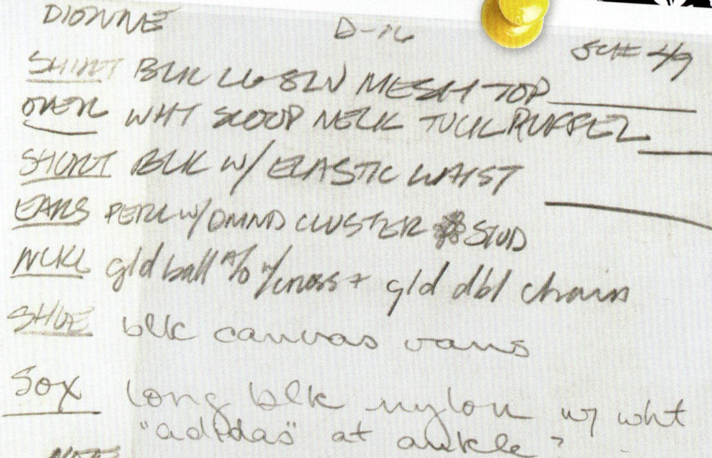

DIONNE D-16 SCN 49

SHIRT BLK LG SLV MESH TOP

OVER WHT SCOOP NECK TUCK RUFFLE

SHORT BLK w/ ELASTIC WAIST

EARS PERL w/ DMND CLUSTER STUD

NCKL gld ball w/ cross + gld dbl chain

SHOE blk canvas vans

SOX long blk nylon w/ wht "adidas" at ankle?

NOTE

AMBER SCN 49 D-16

TANK BLK/WHT STRIPE w/ RED STAR OMO RED TRIM COLLER

JCK BLK FITTED LYCRA w/ SLV STRIPES/STARS

SHORTS BLK/WHT STRIPES

SOX THICK COT. OVER THE KNEE

SHOE RED HI TOP "CONVERSE"

EARS CHER'S SLV. HOOPS w/ cir. STAR

NCKL LTHR w/2 STARS SLV. CHOKER

Bracelet SLV w/ STAR Villi (RT)

*PROPS RED BEEPER

NOTE JCK OPEN

"There goes your social life."

JULIE: "I think part of the reason the film is still so popular is because the girls were so self-possessed and looked adorable. It's aspirational. Like, 'I want to be that cool and dress like them.'"

MONA: "You know, Amy really fought to make the girls the center of the movie. Other teen movies were about the boys' experience."

JULIE: "Before *Clueless*, the studios didn't value girl movies. There would be no *Legally Blonde* or even *Barbie* without *Clueless*."

MONA: "Thank you. I love being thought of as a trailblazer for movies about powerful women with amazing costumes!"

Q&A—Mona & Julie:

MONA: "Did you ever think *Clueless* would become such a hit?"

JULIE: "Yes! I knew it as soon as I read the script. It was so smart. And then you created all these amazing costumes that became iconic. For the gym scene, you didn't reflect what kids were wearing. You invented styles that didn't even exist."

MONA: "I'm sorry you had to wear the sweatshirt and tube socks. Gym teachers are not cool, and you grounded that scene by looking like a real person."

JULIE: "I had to accept that my character was not glamorous. Ugh! But I know, from working with you on other projects, that you make women look incredible. You taught me to really appreciate my shape and show my cleavage—but not in *Clueless*."

MONA: "It's so important to highlight your best assets. Know your body shape and show off what you love. Why do you think *Clueless* is still so beloved?"

Style Guide: Let's Get Physical

May and Heckerling decided on a black and white palette to mimic the drab navy and white P.E. looks popular at Catholic high schools. "We always started with a real and grounded base," says May, who then veered into surreal with her creations. Heckerling chimes in: "The costumes are so great because what sport would you actually do in them? They're like gym uniforms on fashion drugs!"

"I knew Amber wasn't going to wear plain old sweatpants," says Donovan, whose outrageous stars and stripes ensemble got even more over the top with her ringlet hair extensions and thigh-high stockings. "These girls look like a chorus line about to break into a dance number," says Heckerling.

Cher opted for a sexy black tank over a classic white tee, which became all the rage after *Clueless*. "I wanted to show that she would confidently mix chic with comfort and high with low. That's total Cher," says May. The gold chain phone purse and custom water bottle holder were accents decades ahead of their time.

For Dionne, May also layered a crisp white dickie with a black leotard and added a classic bandana to set off Dash's box braids. It's clear that Dionne and Cher are besties, just by their complementary style. Don't miss that beeper attached to her gym shorts.

ABOVE: May designed an embellished, Chanel-like cell phone carrying case that added both style and function to Cher's outfits.

PINK

No Sweat: How to Mix Chic and Sporty

When Gucci sends bicycle shorts with tweed jackets and zip-up hoodies over gowns down the catwalk, you know athleisure has hit the big leagues. The upside is fashion designers now recognize our need for comfort. The caveat is how counterintuitive it can be to add sporty pieces to your wardrobe. May, who loves to wear vibrant high-top sneakers, shares her tips for making comfortable pieces look chic.

• Invest in "fashion sneakers": It's cool to pair sporty footwear with tailored pants, a maxi dress, or even a suit. Just make sure these sneakers are pristinely clean.

• Befriend black leggings: A flattering pair of form-fitting but stretchy leggings become the perfect foundation to a look when you add a cardigan, blazer, or belted jacket. Platform booties or heels heighten the fashion quotient.

• Layer for the win: Dress like Cher and layer a spaghetti-strap top over a tee. Don't forget to accessorize with a choker or bold gold chain.

TRANS

CELEBRATING
Fashion
Tai
HIGH SCHOOL

T-SHIRT GRN & WHT STRIPES w/WHT LG SLV.
FULL CIRCLE
OVERSHIRT FOREST GRN LG/SLV
but up 6 TIMES
JEZABEL
SKIRT GRN & WHT PLAID
BLK 5 but's
NECESSARY OBJECTS
Tights olv grn w/SELF STRIPE & PRINT
EARS TINY gld HOOPS w/Tiny Hearts
SHOES CRM SUEDE FLATS w/
WIDE STRAP

"Di, don't you want to use your popularity for a good cause?"

Brittany Murphy once said, "I feel as if the words in a script go from the page through my arm and my body, into my heart, and all of a sudden take me over." Nothing could better describe the late actress' depiction of Tai, an uprooted teen adrift in search of an identity. When Tai shows up to Bronson Alcott High School with her anime-eyes and eager smile, the audience melts like butter on toast. Even Cher can't help but take Tai under her queen bee wing for a well-intentioned but misguided makeover.

"Brittany was so vivacious and had such *joie de vivre* spirit," says May, who outfitted her in baggy, unflattering clothes for her first scene in *Clueless*. "She was like, 'Make me a really ugly duckling now so I can be more beautiful later.'" Heckerling, too, saw in Murphy a powerhouse who could play soft and hard: "Brittany had a vulnerability at her core, but when she looks at Cher and says, 'You're a virgin who can't drive,' I got chills."

Every *Clueless* cast member interviewed for this book paused and spoke emotionally when Murphy's name came up. The actress passed away in 2009, more than 16 years ago, but she's as memorable as the movie itself

MALE ☐ FEMALE ☒

SHOW TITLE: Clueless
JOB NUMBER:
CAST:
CHARACTER: TAI

CHANGE NO.	SCENE NO.	EXT. INT. SET	D N	COSTUME DESCRIPTION
1 49 To 54		X FALL		PANT BRN BAGGIES SHOE YELLOW W/WHT STRIPE PUMA NOTE SHIRT OPEN DROPS BACK PACK
	49	GYM	D/16	
	50	LUNCH COURT		
	51-52	FOOD LINE		
	53 54	CHER HOUSE		

Brittany was a force! At 17 years old, she knew exactly how the character should look and feel. In our first fitting Brittany said, "Let's make Tai look helpless so when I arrive in school, Cher would feel really sorry for me." That gave me a great start for the makeover. We had so much fun creating the character and finding Tai's final, self-assured look by the end of the film. Brittany was a terrific artist and I loved working with her!!

Mona May

In Memory of Brittany

DONALD FAISON: "She was such a positive force. And she could get completely lost in a character, which isn't easy. I learned a lot about acting from Brittany."

BRECKIN MEYER: "Brittany was like a little sister to me. In the wedding scene in the end, I was supposed to kiss her on the mouth, but I kissed her on the forehead instead."

ELISA DONOVAN: "I remember Brittany like a hummingbird, fluttering and magical. She had an energy that always made you feel like she was ecstatic to see you. Fiercely talented, in a raw-nerve sort of way. Her heart and soul on her sleeve. I felt oddly protective of her. For as powerful as she was, she seemed fragile.

NICOLE BILDERBACK: "Brittany Murphy was always smiling. Her big, beautiful ball of energy was infectious. You couldn't help but to smile when she was around and no one could light up a room like she did."

JEREMY SISTO: "Brittany was awesome. So fun, and pure, and enthusiastic. I would see her for years at parties and clubs, and we always had a great connection. An amazing person."

AMY HECKERLING: "Brittany would surprise you as an actress when she showed this strong side. You would think she was soft, and you wouldn't expect it at all. I have the silver combat boots she wore in one scene, but I would never wear them. They are my Brittany memento."

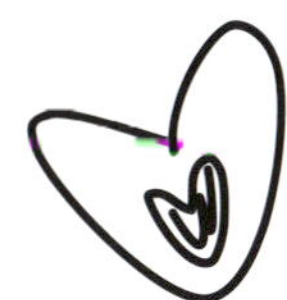

PAUL RUDD: “She could be heartbreaking and funny simultaneously. In that scene where she gets hit in the head with the shoe at the party, she doesn’t oversell it. She just drops out of the frame. She was innately good at what she did.”

ALICIA SILVERSTONE: “In the audition for Tai, I remember thinking, ‘I need to tell them it has to be Brittany.’ But then, of course, it was like, ‘Duh. They know.’ Her talent wasn’t a secret.”

TWINK CAPLAN: “Brittany was such a deep and warm-hearted girl. She didn’t drive. So whenever we had a party or some type of celebration, she would ask if she could bring her mother, Sharon.”

STACEY DASH: “When Cher and I include Tai and make her our new friend, it was genuine. She was so sweet.”

Style Guide: Tai Finds Herself

Tai shows up during gym class, wearing oversized jeans with a baggy, plaid button-down atop a Treasure Troll tee shirt. She's a poster girl for grunge—and wears clothes most kids in America favored in the mid-'90s. Amber snidely comments: "She could be a farmer in those clothes." Cher, however, sees a damsel in a distressing outfit and decides to make Tai over.

Tai's transformation montage shows Cher and Dionne starting from square one: They strip away the garish Manic Panic dye from her hair, line her big brown eyes, add a pink pout, and most importantly, dress her up in a cute feminine outfit: a mini skirt with a fitted shirt, emblazoned with a heart. It's almost as if they sculpt a female form out of clay. "You can see they want her to be as girly as possible," says May.

When Tai becomes Cher's fashion doppelganger, her attitude changes, too. She's no longer the lovable underdog. "What brought on this surge of empowerment?" Cher asks Tai, and you see her discomfort with this new confident version of Tai. When Tai says the famous line, "You're a virgin who can't drive," she's acting as judgemental as Cher when she puts down Amber and Travis.

Finally, in the skateboard park scene, Tai embraces her true self. She's decked out in the female surfer lifestyle brand Roxy and wears her hair in tomboy braids that show off her face. "You can tell that Tai is totally comfortable here with who she is and what she's wearing," says May. "I love this look because it's Tai's real self and she looks so happy."

ABOVE: Tai blossoms into her most authentic self by the end of the film, and the costumes May designed supported Tai's journey along the way. "Don't let anyone tell you who you are," says May. "You need to figure it out for yourself."

Change It Up

Tai shows us the number one rule of makeovers: Don't lose sight of your inner-self. A style transformation—whether it's a wardrobe refresh or a new hairstyle—should complement your personality and simplify your lifestyle. Case in point: When Cher remakes Tai into a polished mirror image of herself, Tai forfeits her free spirit and love of streetwear. Think of your own upgrade as a "give and take-over" instead of a makeover.

May advises you start by trying new accessories or a new shade of lipstick. Then, if you're still in a rut with, say, your classic look, add some grit with a studded purse or a motorcycle jacket. If you're already edgy, experiment with more refined pieces like a tweed boucle jacket or pearls. "Honor your core look and play with opposite possibilities for contrast," says May.

SANDRO
PURSE

RESO
Designe

NATE
Fashion
HISTORY
looks

Nowadays, fashion and Hollywood are fast friends. Designers vie to get their looks in films, while actresses with brand relationships request to wear specific clothes onscreen. YSL recently produced its first movie; Tom Ford directs features. But in 1995, there was no such synergy. May, who had studied fashion in New York and Paris, knew which designers would resonate with the audience—and also, "pop" on the big screen. "The script talked about the fashion being important, but I had to determine which looks from the European runways these girls would embrace. They had the money to shop their way down Rodeo Drive," she says.

Heckerling, a woman who doesn't follow fashion or even love getting dressed in the morning, trusted her costume designer implicitly. Unfortunately, May didn't have the budget to buy outfits off the runway. "I begged," she says of her appeal to Azzedine Alaia to let her borrow the perfect knit, body-con red dress Cher wears when she gets mugged in a parking lot. "Then, I had to tell him that she would wear that dress when she has to get on her knees. Not an easy conversation to have, but he was wonderful about it," says May with a laugh. She also managed to convince designers like Calvin Klein, Anna Sui, Jill Stuart, and Dolce & Gabbana to loan special pieces. The rest is (fashion) history.

"You don't understand. This is an Alaia!"

THESE PAGES: The Christmas party in the Valley called for dressier looks. May loved taking everyone's style up a few notches and creating a festive holiday palette with costumes. She even outfitted Producer Adam Schroeder as a party guest.

Clueless
'Cher'
Christmas Party
Felipe Sanchez

Style Guide: Anatomy of the Red Alaia Look

In a throng of Christmas party revellers, Cher has to be the focal point. May achieved that by putting Silverstone in a stop-sign-red Alaia dress that clung to her every curve. "This is a grown-up moment for Cher because she's sexier than we have seen her in the film so far," says May. "You know she's the leading lady on screen."

The late Tunisian fashion designer Azzedine Alaia, who invented the bandage dress in the mid-'80s, celebrated the female form with stretch and structure. His knit creations have been spotted on countless red carpets and style icons, from Madonna to Rihanna. "Only a teen who followed the runways would know an Alaia," says May.

Cher's dress, a seamed mini with a square neckline and criss-cross back, moves with her when she hits the dance floor at the party. She highlights her bare shoulders by wearing her hair in a topknot and accentuates her pout with matching red lipstick.

May designed an elegant, belted evening jacket for Cher, using rich red jacquard fabric and black raven feathers. "It was perfect because she dramatically unveils the dress when she walks into the party," says May, who added a peplum waist for even more oomph.

For accessories, May created a feathered purse to carry Cher's "red lipstick and credit card" and chose sexy, red satin heels. "They are still Mary Janes though, because Cher is innocent," says May.

BELOW: Dating back to the 1960s, the creepy 32-foot-high neon clown sign for a liquor store in North Hollywood makes the perfect backdrop for when Cher gets mugged.

AUTHENTIC Style
Let's

VIBE
Party

"Sometimes, I have more fun vegging out than when I go partying. Maybe because my party clothes are so binding."

Every teen movie has its requisite party scene. Heckerling wanted to get the vibe right in *Clueless*, so she hit a few L.A. high school soirees on the sly. "Somebody would take me to a kegger and I would go, 'What's with all the beer? And why are people throwing quarters into glasses?'" she recalls with a laugh.

Clueless features two parties: the Christmas bash in the Valley and the college party, where Tai tumbles down the stairs as ska band The Mighty Mighty Bosstones play live onstage. "We didn't have a lot of commercial success before Clueless. The song we performed in the film got some college radio play before that, but most people who recognize those songs recognize them from the movie," lead singer Dicky Barret has said. (FYI: The band disdained playing at a "frat party," so Heckerling revised the script to make it a "college party.")

For costume designer May, the biggest challenge was upholding the *Clueless* world by dressing every single extra: "No one wore their own clothes because they all showed up in the dark, baggy grunge look of that time. I needed each one to be part of the color palette in this capsule world we created." The payoff? A realistic and aesthetic window into how kids socialize when adults aren't around.

THESE PAGES: Call it a coincidence: Ska punk band the Mighty Mighty Bosstones also had a penchant for plaid. The group later commented that the actors in *Clueless* struggled a bit to dance to their "reggae on steroids" beats.

1-4
1-8
1-3
1-7
1-2
1-6

Style Guide: Anatomy of Tai's Fashion Montage

When Tai shows up to the college party, she immediately tumbles down a set of stairs and announces, "Now, all night long, I'm going to be known as that girl who fell on her butt." To punctuate Tai's discomfort, May outfitted her in an outfit that could be reinterpreted: "Tai feels like she's not pretty enough or cool enough—and no one is paying attention to her. So, she starts playing with her outfit."

It's obvious that Tai has been styled by Cher in her patchwork overalls, bright pink top, and sheer patterned shirt. May created the mismatched look so that Tai could change up the separates in a montage.

- First, Tai ties the shirt around her waist. Hmm. Not working.

- Maybe the shirt could be jerry-rigged into a headband? No way.

- Finally, she ties the shirt around her waist. It's the equivalent of raising a white flag in defeat.

It's no coincidence that The Mighty Mighty Bosstones play their hit, "Where'd You Go?" during the Tai montage. Clearly, Tai has tried on a new identity, and it's as ill-fitting as her clothes.

Her silver Doc Martens are the only nod to Tai's authentic style. "She's really only comfortable in her combat boots," says May.

FUN FACT:
Extras make more money for kissing on camera. Heckerling asked a guy and girl if they wanted to make out during the Valley party scene. They agreed. Years later, the two stopped her the street. "Hey Amy! We're engaged now. Thank you."

EMPOW
And then there were
COORDINATING
Outfits

"Amy Heckerling was a trailblazer for people like me to be seen—as I am—and normalized it on the big screen. Throughout the years, I've had multiple strangers walk up to me to tell me that I was the only representation in TV and film they had growing up. It's brought me to tears when I think of the impact this movie has had worldwide. I'm forever grateful to Amy Heckerling for opening that door."

—NICOLE BILDERBACK

Teen girls travel in packs and typically dress alike. When we see the miniskirt-clad trio of Cher, Dionne, and Tai walking in a line at school, they scream "clique"—but still stand apart from each other in their coordinating outfits. That's no accident. May cycled through dozens of looks that flatter the three leads separately and as a group. The intention is always to define each character in her respective arc within the story. "Here is where you see Tai as a true mini-Cher with her plaid skirt. But she's wearing a more muted palette, and she's not as polished," says May. "You can easily decipher the social pecking order by their clothes."

Offscreen, there was no such hierarchy. The actresses all bonded and looked out for each other, says Twink Caplan, who played teacher Miss Geist and acted as an impromptu "den mother" to the young cast. (Caplan, a long-time collaborator with Heckerling, also co-produced *Clueless*.) "The girls all had this camaraderie because it was their opportunity to soar," she adds. "And Amy let them play these roles in their own way, so they felt empowered on set." Dash sums it up simply: "Amy didn't write these young ladies to be bitchy—and we weren't."

"Wow, you guys talk like grownups."

OPPOSITE: Summer stood out for her love of layering shirts and OMG hair accessories, like the reindeer she wore in her pigtails at the Christmas party. Her costumes are equally inspired by Harajuku style and '90s rave culture.

Style Guide: Who Runs the World? Girls.

Tai's copycat version of Cher's iconic look—plaid mini with a green cardigan—is giving more suburban mall than Paris runway. "You know that Tai doesn't have the money to duplicate Cher's wardrobe, and it shows," says May. It's also clear that Cher has styled Tai as her mirror image.

Dash name-checks this burgundy velvet costume as her favorite look in the film: "I looked so smart and elegant in that outfit. I still think about it. I definitely would wear it today." May envisioned a high school girl wearing French cuffs as a wink to European style. She also accessorized Dash with a ladylike 1950s purse.

Cher, in a Brooks Brothers button-down shirt that brings out her blue eyes, looks ready to run for student council president. "She's always in charge, and it shows," says May, who completed the preppy power look with a Fair Isle pullover knit vest, pearl earrings, and a vintage brown snap-up suede skirt.

THESE PAGES: "Oh my God, do you see how boys are responding?!" Cher exclaims as she and Dionne debut Tai's new look.

NAIR
Fashion
RULES OF ATTRACTION

"He does dress better than I do."

In our first glimpse of Cher's high school crush, debonair Christian leans against a classroom doorway with his jacket insouciantly slung over his shoulder. He smoulders like a modern-day James Dean in high-waisted, belted gabardine pants with a fitted black tee that accentuates his physique. "With all the boys in baggy clothes, I wanted Cher to be attracted to this suave guy from a different era," says Heckerling, who has a thing for retro gangster types. May particularly loved how Heckerling deftly wrote a queer character without indulging in stereotypes—and created a cool cat, vintage look for him. "He's super stylish and masculine, but we don't know he's gay until the actual reveal," she says. Also, Christian, played by actor Justin Walker, doesn't just dress the part of a Rat Packer. He speaks in mid-century slang, using expressions like "nice stems" and "I dig."

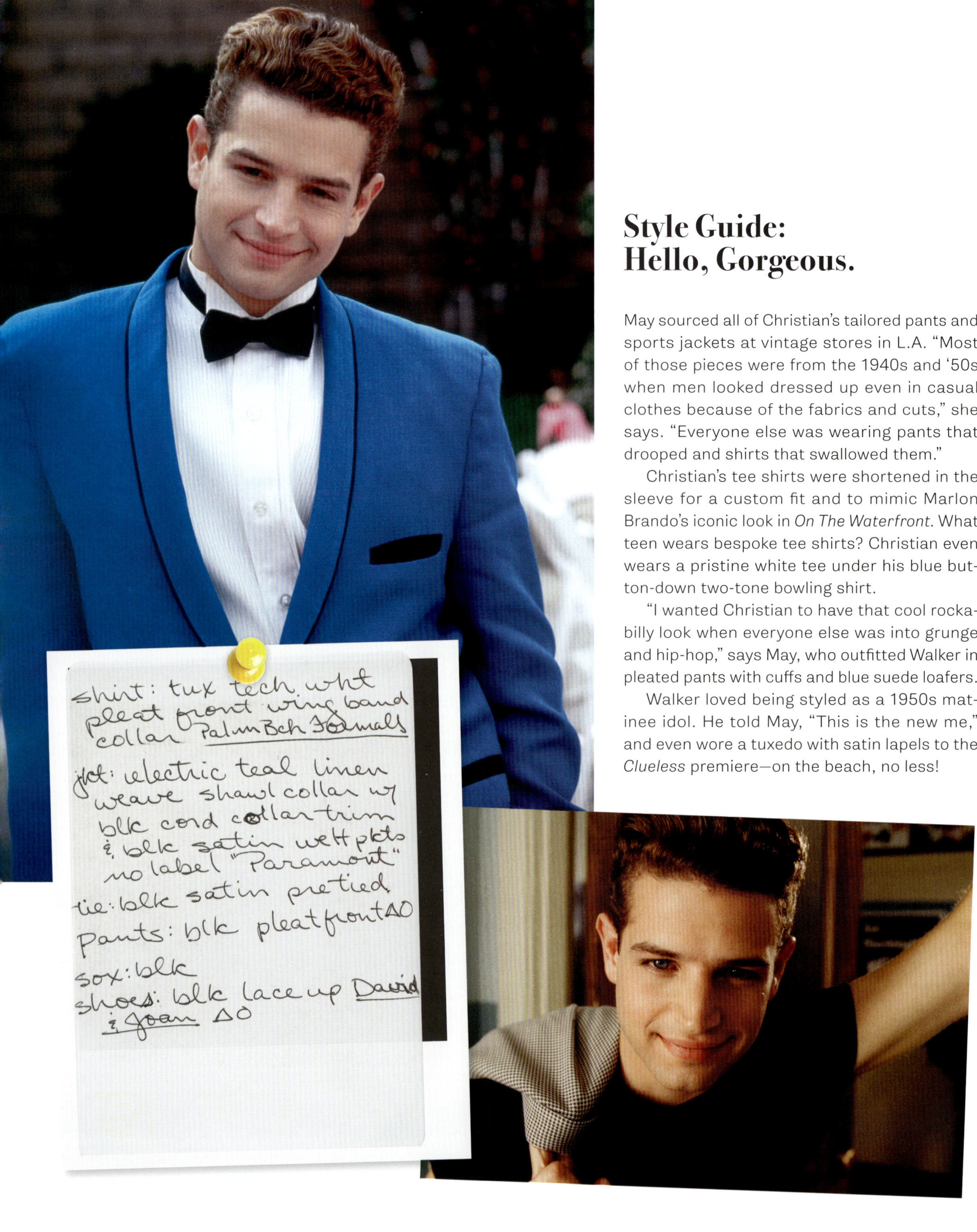

Style Guide: Hello, Gorgeous.

May sourced all of Christian's tailored pants and sports jackets at vintage stores in L.A. "Most of those pieces were from the 1940s and '50s when men looked dressed up even in casual clothes because of the fabrics and cuts," she says. "Everyone else was wearing pants that drooped and shirts that swallowed them."

Christian's tee shirts were shortened in the sleeve for a custom fit and to mimic Marlon Brando's iconic look in *On The Waterfront*. What teen wears bespoke tee shirts? Christian even wears a pristine white tee under his blue button-down two-tone bowling shirt.

"I wanted Christian to have that cool rockabilly look when everyone else was into grunge and hip-hop," says May, who outfitted Walker in pleated pants with cuffs and blue suede loafers.

Walker loved being styled as a 1950s matinee idol. He told May, "This is the new me," and even wore a tuxedo with satin lapels to the *Clueless* premiere—on the beach, no less!

Style Guide: Cher's Guide to Flirting

One classroom montage in *Clueless* could be described as a masterclass in luring a mate. Right after Cher opines, "Searching for a boy in high school is as useless as searching for meaning in a Pauley Shore movie," she spots Christian. Let's cycle through some of Cher's fashion rules of attraction.

In one scene, Cher purposefully drops her pen with a pink feather pom-pom cap on the floor so Christian can glimpse her bare legs as he retrieves it. Was that calculated? Hell, yes. "Cher sees everything as an accessory that has to match her outfit," says May.

Nothing lends mystery like a different hairstyle every day of the week. Cher wears her blonde tresses in a chic '60s-inpired half-up style, a frisky high ponytail and sideswept waves as she vies for Christian's attention in the classroom.

Cher says "Also, sometimes you have to show a little skin. This reminds guys of being naked and then they think of sex"—and backs up her advice by wearing spaghetti strap slip dresses in white eyelet and floral silk edged with lace that bare her shoulders. "But she still looks innocent!" insists May.

Something Old. Something New.

For men, vintage pieces like a suit jacket or cardigan can elevate a basic look like jeans and a tee or create a more distinctive silhouette. One fun and easy way to determine which era suits your taste and physique is to watch classic movies for inspo. Steve McQueen in *The Thomas Crown Affair* epitomizes mod 1960s style, while every character in *Do the Right Thing* shows off a sporty '80s New York vibe. A simple way to pepper your wardrobe with vintage flair is to start with accessories and classic separates like retro Persol sunglasses, pork pie hats or fedoras, preppy cardigans, and trench coats. "Ease into an era rather than overly embrace the look of that time," says May.

ABOVE: James Dean made the tight white T-shirt a classic masculine staple for men, while the Rat Pack (Sinatra and friends) strongly endorsed slim-cut suits with skinny ties and stingy-brim fedoras.

FEDORA

BELO
Fashion FIX
Cher
and

OVED
Calvin

When Cher descends the grand stairway in an itsy-bitsy white slip of a dress for her first date with Christian, it's Josh who really swoons. "I knew I had to push the envelope in this scene because the script has Cher wearing something inappropriate like a negligee," says May. (The scene is a sly nod to the classic 1958 musical *Gigi*.) After a dozen fittings with mini dresses and short skirt sets, the simple snow-white Calvin Klein slip dress fit the bill for Silverstone's character. It's racy and revealing, but still innocent.

Hecklerling's favorite beat in the date scene is Cher's fashion fix when her dad tells her to cover up: "She comes back downstairs with a completely see-through shirt. It's hysterical, thanks to Mona," says the director. Anna Sui designed the diaphanous sheer duster. The Calvin Klein dress remained so beloved that the brand's creative director Francisco Costa procured the original pattern from Italy and reissued the sexy frock fifteen years later in 2010. It sold out. Ultimately, May's challenge as a costume designer was to create sexy looks for Cher without baring too much skin. "She's 16, so she never looks inappropriate," she says.

BELOW: Cher drives a "loc'd out" white 1994 Jeep Wrangler, but Christian's stylish, bright yellow 1954 Nash Metropolitan steals the show.

"What the hell is that?"

How to Wear Pastels

Forget every rule you have heard about wearing pastels. No, they're not just for summer. Yes, you can wear white as formalwear. Here are a few tips for donning a light, bright neutral.

- Invest in a LWD, a little white dress that works with heels or ballet flats. Or consider a white suit.
- Stock up on veneer-white ribbed tanks and tees that pair perfectly with faded jeans or high-waisted white pants.
- Ecru, or off-white, is a softer shade that warms up any skin tone.

Style Guide: Cher's First Date 'Fit

Like Heckerling, May also adores the sequence in which Cher's dad calls her dress "underwear". "Then she comes back down wearing a sheer shirt by Anna Sui that doesn't cover anything," says Mona, with a laugh.

Cher opts for minimal accessories for her first date. May added a crystal flower necklace by L.A. jewelry designer Tarina Tarantino that complemented Silverstone's fair skin tone and the pristine dress.

The white dress and matching patent leather Mary Janes subliminally allude to Cher's lack of sexual experience. "We know she's a virgin, and this look feels pure and almost like a teen version of a wedding dress," says May.

Later, we see Cher at the college party, and she stands out on the dark dance floor in her simple short white dress. Other than Amber, wearing a tiered pink vintage skirt and her hair in a towering beehive, Cher is the most dressed up in a crowd of casually dressed students.

ABOVE: "I can't just open it; I have to make him wait awhile!" Cher always knows how to make an entrance.

FASC

Cher seduces Christian

Sophisticated DATE NIGHT

NATE

On the night Cher invites her crush over to watch a movie, we see prep that includes creating side-swept hair, applying bold makeup, baking cookies, and slipping into a kitten-soft, hot-pink velvet dress. May relied on mini dresses with spaghetti straps to collude with the character's seduction plan. "Cher is sixteen, so she associates pink with love," says the costume designer, who scored this dress off the rack.

ABOVE: Cher's seduction of Christian includes a culinary fiasco: She throws premade cookies into the oven and scorches them. "Aw honey, you baked," Christian says through the smoke.

". . . Christian is brutally hot. And I'm going to remember tonight forever."

Style Guide: First Date Prep

Eyes: Cher favored a subtle rich brown eyeliner most days, but make-up supervisor Alan Friedman opted for striking black liner to accentuate her sky-blue eyes for date night. "We also went for fake lashes, which she didn't wear during the day," he says. He swept a swath of pink eyeshadow on her lids to complement Cher's eyes and pink dress.

Lips: Friedman wanted her pout to pop on the big night: "To make Cher's look stand out from her neutral palette of pinky-nude lips, I picked a bright fuchsia shade."

Cheeks: Again, Friedman heightened the overall effect with rosier blush. The idea was to emulate how a teen would do her makeup to look sexier and more adult for an important night: add more of everything.

Mane: Hairstylist Nina Paskowitz swept Cher's hair to the side for a sophisticated date night look. "Then I went into my bag of tricks and found that rhinestone clip," she says. The touch of sparkle lends a little Cinderella vibe to the scenes. A decade later, Paskowitz worked with actress Amanda Bynes as the hairstylist on *She's the Man* and reused the clip in the film. "Amanda loved Clueless and was so excited!" she recalls.

OPPOSITE: Pop culture chronicler David LaChapelle photographed the *Clueless* promo campaign in 1994 in high camp style. "That was an amazing shoot," says Silverstone.

Pretty in Pink

Friedman had just a week to prep the beauty looks for the cast. He met with everyone on the Friday before filming started on Monday! For Cher, he mostly relied on a discontinued MAC matte lipstick in a pinkish-nude called "Malt" with the lipliner "Raisin" (also, no longer available) or "Spice," which is still in stock. "Alicia looks natural for most of the movie, but I made her makeup more dramatic for the date nights and party scenes," says Friedman. "You adjust for lighting and crowds."

PRO TIP:

If you're experimenting with new makeup or absolutely love the effect of a particular shadow or highlighter, take detailed notes of your products and techniques for future reference. "It saves so much time and makes it easy to quickly replicate a look," says Friedman, who refers to the cosmetic CliffsNotes as a "glam and slam."

OBSE
Cher
can't
drive

SSED
CASUAL
Chic
FENDI

"Where's my white collarless shirt from Fred Segal? It's my most capable-looking outfit."

Set mostly in iconic Beverly Hills, *Clueless* is a teenage love letter to Los Angeles. The film spotlights varied neighborhoods almost as much as its characters. Cher shops on Rodeo Drive, parties in the San Fernando Valley and cruises down a freeway with her friends. What more could a cool adolescent want from a city?

"This city has its own distinctive look when it comes to fashion because of the weather, the beach, and the fact that everyone is so active," says May of casual chic and the pastel palette. Here, there are no rules: You can wear white all year round, denim fronts as formalwear, and no one bats an eye if you don a bikini to Starbucks. Cher even name-checks L.A. retailer Fred Segal, a fashion institution that opened in 1961. The boutique quickly became ground zero for the effortless West Coast look and doubled as a hot spot for celebrities. It also launched quintessential SoCal brands like Juicy Couture, designer denim Earl Jeans, and Hard Candy Cosmetics. Elle Woods even mentions Fred Segal in *Legally Blonde*.

But Hollywood is a sartorial study in contrast too: There's a film premiere on any given night with a requisite red carpet. It's not unusual to spot an actress wearing a ball gown as she exits a limousine on Sunset Boulevard. Meanwhile, just a few yards away, a guy dressed as Spiderman in a threadbare costume solicits tourists for paid photo ops. "I hate the sun," Heckerling has said. Nevertheless, she perfectly captured the sunny optimism of Southern California in *Clueless*.

Style Guide: Front Seat Fashion

"I love that Cher's most capable look is a see-through top," says May, who put Silverstone in a sheer tuxedo shirt with an argyle mini skirt. "In her mind, this is a grown-up look."

May layered a baby blue knit vest over Cher's ensemble to show that she's coming undone. It's easily her least put-together look. "For once, Cher can't manipulate the situation and pass the driver's test," she says.

Cher matches her block-heel silver Mary Janes—just one of the five different pairs she wears in the film—with a shiny metallic backpack.

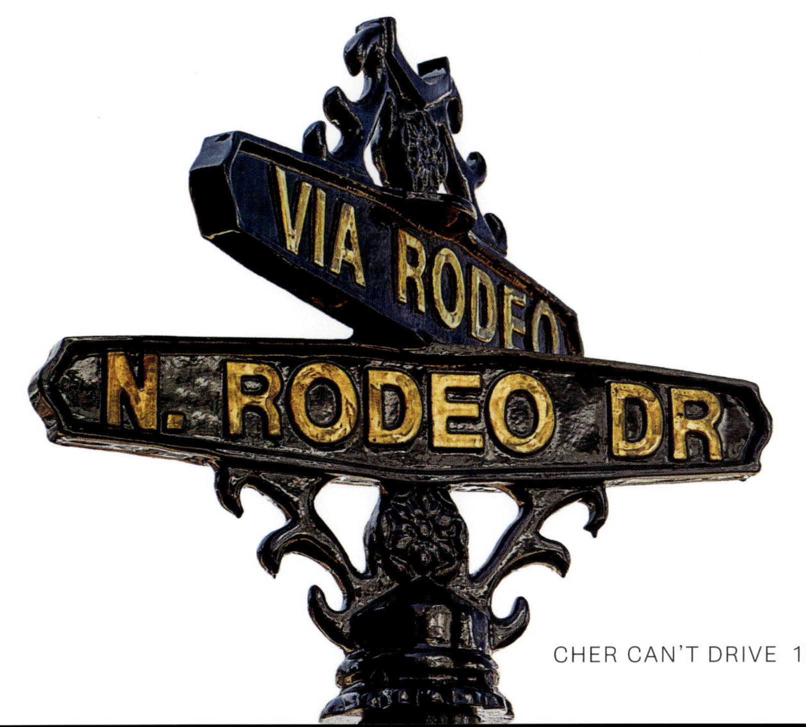

EVOLU
Make me

UTION
THE ART OF COSTUME Design
over

"I decided I needed a complete makeover. Except this time, I makeover my soul."

Make Me Over

When Cher realizes she's the center of her own narrow universe, her costumes mimic her existential crisis. "It's so exciting to play with a color palette and silhouettes to show a character's emotion and depth," says May. "That is truly the art of costume design." Case in point: If you were to watch *Clueless* without sound, you could trace the arc of Cher's narrative through the evolution of her outfits. Her color choices alone veer from "look at me" hues like neon yellow and traffic-light red to shades that harmonize with the human landscape. She wears sneakers—gasp!—and unadorned denim. She even foregoes accessories and sullies her honey-blonde hair. Heckerling craftily upends the makeover trope in *Clueless* by reversing it: A privileged princess puts less emphasis on her appearance and possessions in the end. Who can forget the scene where Cher donates her downhill skis and tennis racquets to victims of the Pismo Beach disaster? Let's hear it for the soul makeover.

LEFT: It's easy to mistake the layout of outdoor lunch tables at Cher's high school for a runway at Paris Fashion Week. That's intentional!

55

Style Guide: Cher Gets Real

"Cher is totally in control when we first meet her," says May. "Her outfits are tailored and match perfectly." The palette she wears—from yellow to pink to pastel green—also telegraphs a sunny naivete about life.

When Cher falls for Christian, she relies on her looks and sexier clothes to attract him. Her skirt suits are traded in for revealing mini dresses. "She's using traditional feminine tactics like dropping her pen and sending herself flowers to seduce him," says May.

In the scene where Tai confronts Cher over her feelings for Josh, our leading teen sees her mirror image reflected back at her—and starts to question her own superficiality. In the next scene, we see a Cher that's stripped down to jeans and a pink tank over a tee. "Her looks are softer because she's no longer so sure of herself," says May.

As Cher pivots from materialist to activist, she wears more simple, casual clothes and a muted palette of blues and greys. "Her hair isn't perfect and she's not carrying a coordinating purse," says May of the slate-hued cardigan and dress she wears at the Pismo Beach fundraiser. "Her designer clothes are no longer her armor or identity."

ABOVE: "Daddy, some people lost all their belongings. Don't you think that includes athletic equipment?" Cher always knows how to put Mel in his place.

ROMA
Harmonious LOOKS
The look of
love

NTIC

"You think I'm beautiful?"

Are you saying you care about me?" Josh asks Cher on the grand staircase. This charming exchange shows the two professing more than just physical attraction. It's clear they accept each other's flaws and inherent differences. May intentionally outfitted Cher in an unfussy look: a romantic eyelet blouse with purple seersucker pedal pushers and sneakers. "The square neckline was perfect for the closeups because this scene is about their vulnerability together and you need to see that in their faces," says May. Josh, too, wears a softer palette of blues and greys. He's let down his guard. May adds: "When the camera pulls back, the two of them look like a real couple. Their costumes don't clash anymore."

OPPOSITE: In the end, it might be equally vain and stylish Amber and Elton who complement each other best.

Style Guide: Do Couples Who Dress Together Stay Together?

On top of creating sychronized BFF costumes, May strengthened the bond between onscreen pairs with "couple clothes" or harmonious looks. Meaning, the characters who dated or had crushes on each other needed to complement each other. "That doesn't mean they match. It means they don't clash," says May.

Dionne and Murray would probably win "best dressed to impress" as a pair. While Dionne favors classic feminine looks and Murray leans into trendy streetwear, the two love bold colors like turquoise, purple, and bright green—and look-at-me hats. "They are both into fashion and very confident about their style. You can imagine them being excited to see what the other one is wearing at school or a party," says May.

Tai and Travis mesh when they wear similar looks like flannels, graphic tees, and cargo pants. When they first meet in the cafeteria, it's as if they share a closet. But when Cher elevates Tai's outfits to preppy, polished skirt sets, she rejects Travis with an insult. Later, when Tai finds her true self and they reunite at the skatepark, her striped Union Bay tee and brown Dickie pants with a bulky silver belt buckle coordinate with Travis' sporty, skate punk look.

Cher's style evolution syncs up with her crushes. When she's way into elegant and sophisticated Christian, she pays extra close attention to her makeup, hair, and outfits. It's all about flirty frocks and a pink pout. But once she admits she loves Josh, she pivots to casual jeans, sneakers, and sweater sets. She also foregoes the updos and makeup for a more earnest and all-natural look. "Cher's priorities shift so she's less fussy and pretentious about her style. She doesn't copy Josh, but she focuses less on her appearance," says May.

Something told me not to discount Miss Geist.

FUN FACT: Paris Hilton once approached Caplan at a Hollywood party in the '90s to say, "Miss Geist is hot!" Caplan agreed. "Paris is actually shy and very sweet," she says.

How Miss Geist Becomes a Bombshell

Cher and Dionne play matchmaker to Miss Geist (Twink Caplan) and Mr. Hall (Wallace Shawn) for one selfish reason: to get better grades. When we first meet the teacher, she's wearing a huge shirt with a clownish collar and a frumpy skirt with her slip peeking out at the hem. She's adorably unkempt. There's even a run in her stockings. All of that is calculated to show that Miss Geist is lost in her own world.

"Mona knows exactly how to hone in and help you get into character. She puts you in the costume, and she takes pictures. You discuss the looks before she shares them with the director. It's a true creative process between the costume designer and the actor," says Caplan. To transform Miss Geist in a way that feels organic, May gave the character snug pencil skirts that accentuated her figure and dressed her in colors that brightened her complexion. You're watching a flower bloom. "It's not that she's unrecognizable after her makeover. It's that she cares about how she looks because she sees beyond her little world. She also radiates because she's in love," says May.

Clueless
TWINK
MISS GEIST
COSTUME DESCRIPTION
SPILLS COFFEE
STAIN ON DRESS?

ELEG
Finale
and

Love IS IN THE AIR

"I am only 16 . . . and this is California not Kentucky!"

Clueless comes to a close with a candy-coated love fest. Our characters have not only found themselves, but each other. Miss Geist marries Mr. Hall, as her bridesmaids in pink vouch for romance at any age. Dionne talks about her own future wedding aesthetic—"All my bridesmaids are going to wear sailor hats!"—as Murray rolls his eyes. Travis and Tai share a cute moment, while intellectual Josh shows just how much he loves Cher by speaking her language when he says: "I'm buggin' myself." (Rudd says it took a few takes for him to nail the slang naturally.)

Heckerling recalls the "Easter egg" hue of the final scenes and how it represented renewal and hope: "The movie takes place over the school year and the color palette told the story, too," she says of the autumnal shades (orange, yellow) in the beginning and the darker holiday hues like red and forest green seen at the parties. "It ends with pastels and Mona perfectly captured the 'love is in the air' beautiful and uplifting palette of pinks and whites," she says. For May, it was all about cultivating optimism and inclusion through costumes. "Everyone is happy as individuals and happily together," she says. "Watching it, you should feel joyful, too."

OPPOSITE: May knew how important Miss Geist's wedding scene was to her character's development—so she stood by Caplan to make sure everything was perfect on set. The wedding dress reveals Miss Geist in a new light, showcasing her every curve.

Q&A—Mona and Twink:

TWINK: "One of the producers (Scott Rudin) wanted me to wear a big Mexican-style dress with a huge, ruffled skirt. But I said, 'Miss Geist just had a makeover. She needs to wear something fitted. Besides, every woman wants to look hot at her wedding!' And Mona, doll, you fulfilled my dream!"

MONA: "For me, the inspiration was to see this woman's beautiful hourglass figure and show her as a gorgeous, sophisticated bride. We talked and you wanted a high collar and an open back to show off your shoulder blades. My Croatian seamstress, who was a former architect, was like, 'How do we even build this dress?' It was cut right to your body."

TWINK: "I was a size two and it was so perfectly fitted, OMG I was ecstatic. Every time I got hungry and went to the food table for a snack or lunch, I'd look around to make sure Mona wasn't nearby, and as soon as I reached for a piece of food I'd feel something rub against my back. 'DON'T eat anything! I can't alter this wedding dress.' It was hilarious.

MONA: "I broke the budget on that dress. But it was so important to me that you looked like a vision. The teen girls always looked beautiful. You represented the possibility of being in love for the first time as a middle-aged woman. We pull the curtain and see stunning Miss Geist with rosy cheeks and a gorgeous body wearing her dream wedding dress. And I made you that little fascinator to wear with the rose."

TWINK: "I loved my little headpiece! It was amazing! That's Mona May's signature; she has a gift for knowing exactly how to put whimsy and spirit into her designs. She knew my curves and always dressed me spectacularly, even if I couldn't sit down between takes. Mona got me the slant board actresses like Jean Harlow used back in the 1930s that I could prop myself against."

MONA: "But it was all worth it, right?"

TWINK: "Are you kidding? It was the most spectacular I've ever looked!"

FUN FACT:
A scene of Miss Geist marrying Josh as a dream sequence was shot, where Stacey Dash added the flowers to her hair.

Style Guide: Here Come the Looks

Obviously, most teen movies don't end with a colossal wedding. (Okay, except *Sixteen Candles*.) May couldn't wait to dress the principal cast in formal wear for the final scene. "It was my chance to make everyone look elegant in their own way," she says. "But I also made sure that each girl and guy looked true to their character."

Of course, Amber outdid herself as a bridesmaid. May put her in a frothy pink taffeta dress with petticoats and then took it to another level with accessories. "You would think a pink boa and a fuzzy headband would be enough," says Donovan. "No. I also had strings and strings of long pearls."

"Dionne had to stand out even though it's not her wedding," says Dash with a laugh. Her halter dress with a pleated, poufy floral print skirt gave off classic East Coast country club vibes. Dash decided to ante up the effect by adding flowers to her braids. "I still think that look is spectacular," she adds. Her beau Murray didn't disappoint in his pale blue linen suit, paired with a striped shirt featuring a cool Nehru collar. His Superman bling became an ad hoc necktie.

May designed a ladylike pale pink satin suit for Cher to show that she had stepped into her new mature self. She's the only teen who's not competing for the spotlight. "I love that she looks so feminine, but then she fights for the bouquet," says May, who added a pink flower choker to Cher's look to wink at her innocence. (FYI: Heckerling wears a pink bridesmaid dress that matches Cher's, also designed by May.) Josh left his casual comfort zone by donning a mod slim-cut black suit with a punk rock skinny tie. "Um, I am pretty sure that was the suit I owned and lent out to all my friends," Rudd says. "I felt so cool in that tie!"

For Brittany, May chose a baby blue '60s-inspired shift with a silver choker. "She wasn't a bridesmaid so I put her in a soft color that looked great with her skin and auburn hair," says May. In honor of Cher's misguided but well-meaning makeover, Tai wore a pair of white patent Mary Janes. Travis, on the other hand, went rogue in Bermuda shorts with suspenders, a tee shirt and a clip-on bow tie. Meyer says, "I never wore shorts back then because I was a little stick, but I loved Mona's version of a tuxedo for Travis."

ICONI
Cluele
Legendary COSTUMES
continues

ABOVE: May with her beloved pup, who's a fixture on movie sets. Photo by Andrés Garza.

Epilogue

Clueless may be 30 years old, but its cult status shows no sign of fading. Giddy teen girls still scream "As if!" at Silverstone on the street. The clothes May designed continue to inspire fashion designersand curated costume designers alike. A new musical, adapted for the stage by Heckerling, opened in London in March 2025. All that to say the fashion that made this movie so beloved in 1995—and spawned a TV show, book series, comic, and video game—makes it just as relevant and popular today. So much so that Margot Robbie namechecked it when she envisioned the wardrobe of *Barbie*: "We were saying that the wardrobe in *Clueless,* like, the bar was set so high, and we would really like to do something that is as cool as that."

But no matter the medium or update to the original feature film, one element always remains the same: the iconic costumes. *Clueless* is undeniably the most stylish teen movie ever made. *Women's Wear Daily* recently ranked the film's costumes as some of the most memorable of the century, along with other classics like *Breakfast at Tiffany's* and *The Wizard of Oz*. Cher's yellow plaid skirt set paired with over-the-knee white socks and and Mary Janes will forever be revered by fashion fiends—and imitated in homage to *Clueless* by designers like Dior and Versace. "When I created the costumes for these girls, I knew every look had to be classic *and* timeless so they would never go out of style," says May, who singlehandedly took grunge *off* the map by popularizing a sophisticated and feminine wardrobe. She brought high fashion to high school. "I remember seeing teen girls wear bright colors and flattering silhouettes after *Clueless* came out. I was like, 'Yes! They're dressing up again!'"

Her bold costumes set up hilarious punchlines—"You don't understand! This an Alaia!"—that continue to get quoted and raised the profiles. Not to mention, raised the profiles of fashion designers. "I'm proud that people learned about this amazing European designer Azzedine Alaia because of *Clueless*," says May.

The looks even inspire teens and their moms alike dress like total Bettys. Thanks to May, the aesthetic will forever imprint on pop culture and bridge generations. Why else would Kim Kardashian and her daughter North cosplay as Cher and Dionne on Halloween?

No one, including Heckerling or May, foresaw *Clueless* becoming a blockbuster, but everyone likes to muse on why this movie and the fashion still shine as brightly as it did in 1995. "Everything came together. We trapped lightning in a bottle and we looked so cool," says Meyer, who still has Travis' skateboard in his garage. "It was so cutting edge that people are still dressing the way we did in *Clueless*," says Faison. Dash, who wishes she had her wardrobe from the movie, says, "It was an epic journey and the looks Mona created will forever be iconic." Silverstone sums it up eloquently: "I think young people were hungry for something that represented their spirit at that time. Amy and Mona captured that spirit."

That spirit also revolutionized the teen movie genre. It paved the way for seminal films like *Legally Blonde* and *10 Things I Hate About You*. In *Clueless*, there are no vindictive mean girls or absentee adults. Cher may be privileged, but she's an accessible and comically flawed superhero in her coordinating designer outfits. She shops Beverly Hills like a banshee one day and slyly matchmakes lonely middle-aged teachers the next. Most importantly, all she really wants to do is make everyone around her look good. May says, "That legacy will live on."

Many thanks to my fabulous crew: Chic Gennarelli, Vikki Barrett, and John Doyle.
Mona May

CLUELESS CONTINUES ON 161

Where Are Our Characters Now?

Ever wonder what ever happened to Cher? Did she follow in her dad's footsteps to become a ruthless negotiator or launch an athleisure line? What about Dionne? Are she and Murray still in love—and still bickering? Is Travis the new face of the California sober movement? We asked the cast to share their thoughts on where their characters would be today:

Hello

CHER: "She might be with Josh. Who would break up with Josh? But we all know relationships aren't that easy, so maybe not. Cher still loves fashion, but now she has an eco-chic responsible clothing line. Like, she makes leather out of mushrooms and cactus."

DIONNE: "Oh, she's the editor-in-chief of a great fashion magazine based in London. She's still strong and fierce, but also compassionate. Dionne is pushing boundaries about what we wear and she always looks fabulous."

AMBER: "She's on her third or fourth husband and she's running a very over-the-top fashion line. But by 'running,' I mean she owns it and somebody else is doing all of the work. She's taking a lot of the credit though, of course. Maybe she has some kids running around, dressed just like her."

JOSH: "He and Cher still have a soft spot for each other, but they're probably not together anymore. He doesn't live in L.A. That was never his vibe. He still talks a lot about bands like Band of Horses and Fleet Foxes that he thinks are new, but they're not. He's still crunchy. Wait. I'm describing myself!"

MURRAY: "He's a big famous producer in the music business, finding new talent. But he also puts himself in every video and on every track. Oh and of course, he's married to Dionne."

TRAVIS: "He married Tai and she's taking care of him because he's not making a lot of money with his very tame 'Only Fans' account. He's a dad too and they have a bunch of little skater nuggets."

ELTON: "Works in finance. Divorced. Still looking for his Cranberries CD."

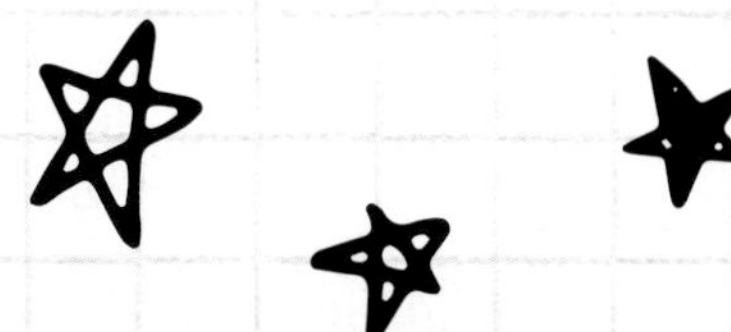

SUMMER: "She's still secretly stealing snowman lawn decor at Christmas and selling them on eBay! Haha!"

MISS GEIST: "She and Mr. Hall have gone the distance. They're still married and they have a menagerie of animals. Every week, they host literature groups in the living room."

MS. STOEGER: "She's running a coffee shop with her girlfriend and maybe coaching on the weekends. She's exactly the same. No personal growth at all."

CLUELESS CONTINUES ON

PO Box 3088
San Rafael, CA 94912
www.insighteditions.com

Find us on Facebook: www.facebook.com/InsightEditions
Follow us on Instagram: @insighteditions

ISBN: 979-8-88663-945-2

Publisher: Raoul Goff
SVP, Group Publisher: Vanessa Lopez
VP, Creative: Chrissy Kwasnik
VP, Manufacturing: Alix Nicholaeff
Art Director: Matt Girard
Designer: Lola Villanueva
Senior Editor: Adrienne Procaccini
Editorial Assistant: Audrey Salo
Executive Managing Editor: Maria Spano
Production Manager: Greg Steffen
Strategic Production Planner: Lina s Palma-Temena

Design inspiration and consultation by YOK Creative

Insight Editions, in association with Roots of Peace, will plant two trees for each tree used in the manufacturing of this book. Roots of Peace is an internationally renowned humanitarian organization dedicated to eradicating land mines worldwide and converting war-torn lands into productive farms and wildlife habitats. Roots of Peace will plant two million fruit and nut trees in Afghanistan and provide farmers there with the skills and support necessary for sustainable land use.

Manufactured in China by Insight Editions

10 9 8 7 6 5 4 3 2 1

Special thanks to:
Risa Kessler / Sabi Lofgren / Eric Lane, Paramount Pictures Mastering Services / Tina Salvador and James Lo, Paramount Digital Post / Allison Bermann, Caitlin Denny, Walter Nolasco, Rebecca Ruud, and Douglas Santos, Paramount Pictures Archives.

Thank you to all the Clueless collaborators: Sherry Lansing, Scott Rudin, Robert Lawrence, Adam Schroeder, Lisa Evans, Isabella Braga, Garet Reilly, Amanda Friedland, Zoya Bergam, Bill Pope, Steven Jordan, Carrie Frazier, Marcia Ross, Debra Chiate, David Kitay, Amy Wells, Richard Graves, Daniel Silverberg, Pat Romano, Esther Vivante, Alan Friedman, Barbara Olivera, Nina Paskovitz, and Geri Oppenheimer.